lonely planet

BARCELONA

Soledad Abella, Mireia Font,
Kyoko Kawaguchi, Joan Torres

Contents

ANDREI BORTNIKAU/SHUTTERSTOCK ©

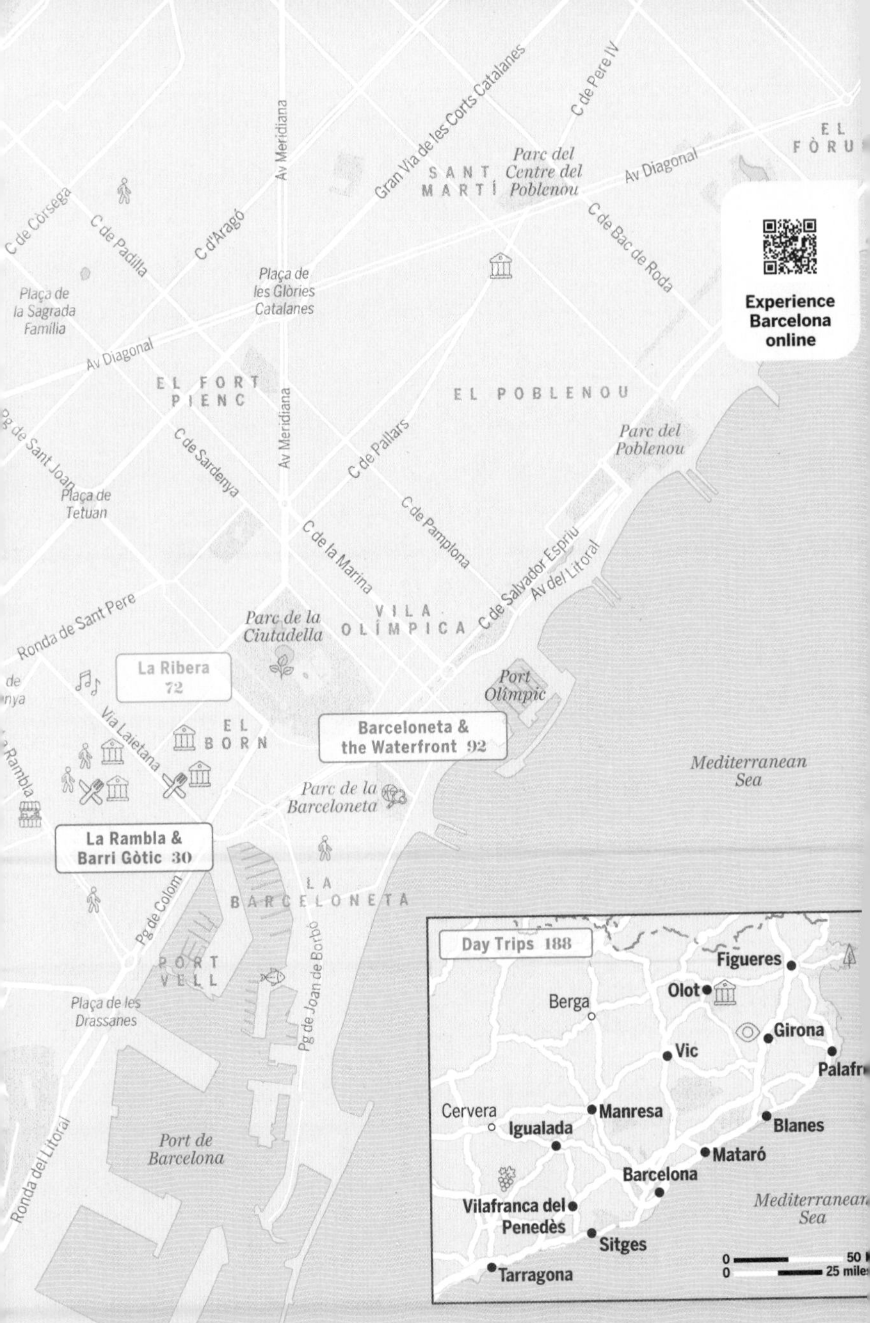

Experience Barcelona online
Gran Via de les Corts Catalanes
C de Pere IV
Av Meridiana
SANT MARTÍ
Parc del Centre del Poblenou
Av Diagonal
EL FÒRU
C de Còrsega
C de Padilla
C d'Aragó
C de Bac de Roda
Plaça de les Glòries Catalanes
Plaça de la Sagrada Família
Av Diagonal
EL FORT PIENC
EL POBLENOU
Pg de Sant Joan
C de Sardenya
Av Meridiana
C de Pallars
Parc del Poblenou
Plaça de Tetuan
C de Pamplona
C de la Marina
C de Salvador Espriu
Av del Litoral
Ronda de Sant Pere
Parc de la Ciutadella
VILA OLÍMPICA
La Ribera 72
Port Olímpic
Via Laietana
EL BORN
Barceloneta & the Waterfront 92
Mediterranean Sea
Parc de la Barceloneta
La Rambla & Barri Gòtic 30
LA BARCELONETA
Pg de Colom
PORT VELL
Pg de Joan de Borbó
Plaça de les Drassanes
Port de Barcelona
Ronda del Litoral
Day Trips 188
Figueres
Olot
Berga
Girona
Vic
Cervera
Manresa
Igualada
Blanes
Mataró
Barcelona
Vilafranca del Penedès
Sitges
Tarragona
Mediterranean Sea
0 50
0 25 miles

Marvel at medieval, modernist and contemporary architecture. Escape to the beach to breathe in the sea breeze and let the sun kiss your skin. Go bar-hopping and taste tapas around the city's culinary hotspots. Stay up late and be part of the local nightlife scene. Experience the power of football at one of the world's most famous stadiums. Explore all forms of art, from museums and galleries to street art. Shop around fancy boulevards. Get lost in old, narrow streets or in bustling markets.

This is Barcelona.

TURN THE PAGE AND START PLANNING YOUR NEXT BEST TRIP →

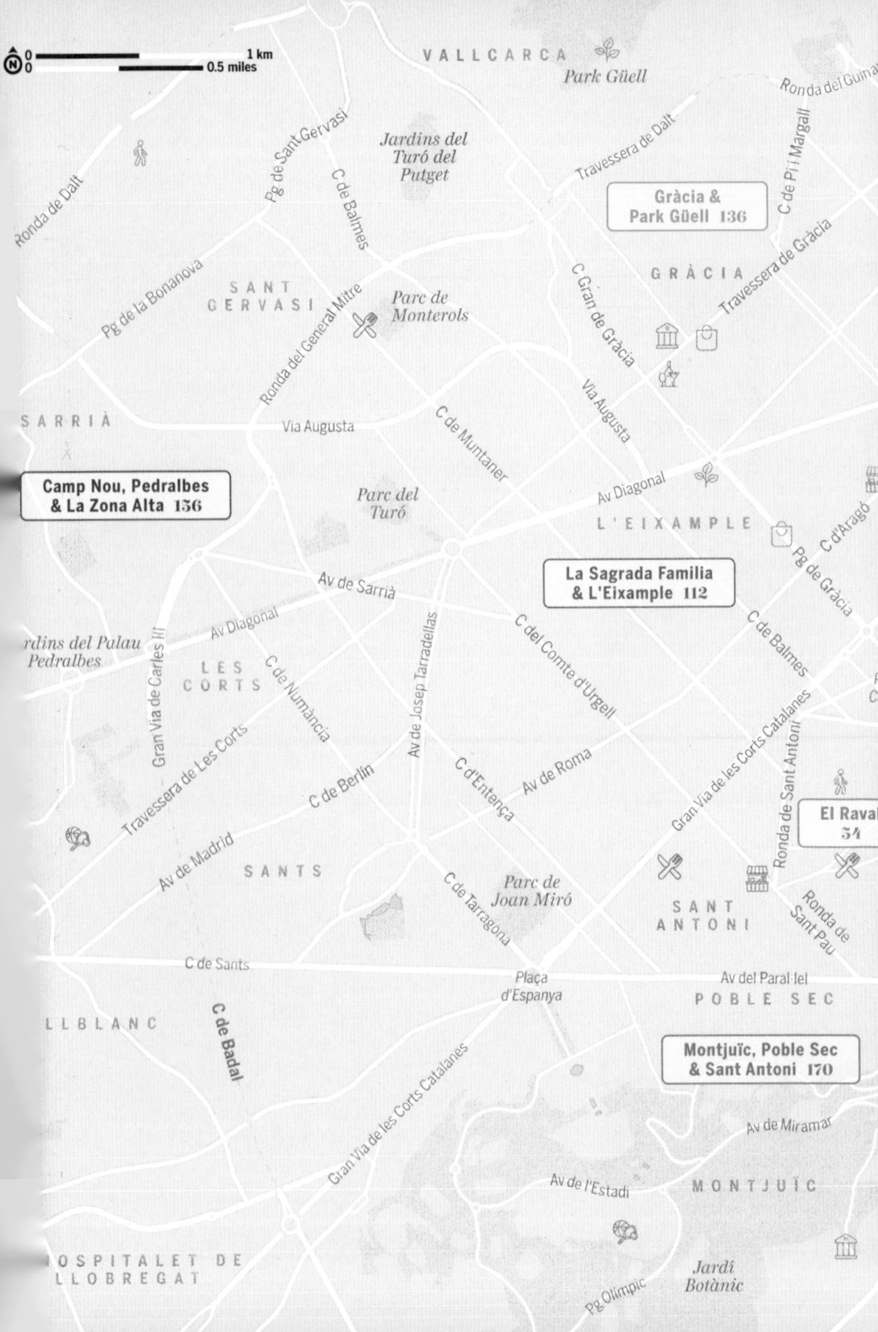

0 1 km
0 0.5 miles
VALLCARCA
Park Güell
Ronda del Guinardó
Jardins del Turó del Putget
Pg de Sant Gervasi
C de Balmes
Travessera de Dalt
C de Pi i Margall
Gràcia & Park Güell 136
Ronda de Dalt
GRÀCIA
Travessera de Gràcia
C Gran de Gràcia
SANT GERVASI
Pg de la Bonanova
Ronda del General Mitre
Parc de Monterols
Via Augusta
SARRIÀ
C de Muntaner
Camp Nou, Pedralbes & La Zona Alta 156
Parc del Turó
Av Diagonal
L'EIXAMPLE
C d'Aragó
La Sagrada Familia & L'Eixample 112
Av de Sarrià
Pg de Gràcia
Av Diagonal
rdins del Palau Pedralbes
C del Comte d'Urgell
C de Balmes
Gran Via de Carles III
LES CORTS
C de Numància
Av de Josep Tarradellas
Gran Via de les Corts Catalanes
Ronda de Sant Antoni
Travessera de Les Corts
C de Berlin
C d'Entença
Av de Roma
El Raval 54
Av de Madrid
SANTS
C de Tarragona
Parc de Joan Miró
SANT ANTONI
Ronda de Sant Pau
C de Sants
Plaça d'Espanya
Av del Paral·lel
POBLE SEC
LLBLANC
C de Badal
Montjuïc, Poble Sec & Sant Antoni 170
Gran Via de les Corts Catalanes
Av de Miramar
Av de l'Estadi
MONTJUÏC
OSPITALET DE LLOBREGAT
Jardí Botànic
Pg Olímpic

Above Panoramic views from Bunkers del Carmel

Day Trips 188

Practicalities 204

ESSAYS

VISUAL GUIDES

WHAT TIME IS DINNER?

When planning to eat out, it's good to keep in mind that locals normally eat lunch between 1pm and 3pm, and dinner between 8.30pm and 10.30pm.

THE CATALAN **MENU**

With an estimated 9000-plus restaurants and bars in the city, Barcelona is definitely a great choice for those who appreciate culinary delights. Food is an important part of life here, whether it's the little everyday moments or celebrating special occasions. The types of food and where you can eat them are so varied in Barcelona; there's something for every palate and every mood.

Left Paella **Right** A variety of tapas
Below Bar Calders (p186), El Raval

→ TAPAS CRAWL

Tapas let you try a little bit of everything. You'll find them everywhere in Barcelona.

CRISTINA PEDRAZZINI/GETTY IMAGES ©

SEAFOOD SPECIALITIES

At a beach bar or in a hectic market, there are plenty of options here for those wanting to taste fresh, delicious seafood.

RIGHT: MERIPOPPS/SHUTTERSTOCK ©
LEFT: ESKYSTUDIO/SHUTTERSTOCK ©

↑ UNUSUAL PAIRINGS

Take a break from tapas and go for something less conventional; try world cuisine in El Raval (p70) or avant-garde restaurants in Sant Antoni (p186).

Best food experiences

- **Go on a culinary adventure in Barcelona's medieval heart – if you don't know where to start, follow the foodies' recommendations** (p50)
- **Taste world cuisine in diverse El Raval** (p70) **or fancy L'Eixample** (p126)
- **Indulge in the freshest seafood in Barceloneta, the city's traditional fishing neighbourhood** (p110)
- **Go bar-hopping on Barcelona's famous *pintxo* (Basque tapas) street, Carrer de Blai** (p186)

FINDING YOUR VIBE

Fanciest spots L'Eixample

Laid-back bars Gràcia

Underground scene El Raval

LGTBIQ+ scene 'Gaixample', around Plaça Universitat

Nightclubs Port Olímpic, Carrer de Tuset, L'Eixample and Barri Gòtic

BUZZING **NIGHTLIFE**

Barcelona is famous for its nightlife and it's no surprise it has been called 'the city that never sleeps'. It's safe to say there's something happening every night of the week, no matter the season. If you're looking for a fun night out, whether it's going for a drink, dancing or enjoying a live concert, you've come to the right place.

CHRISTIAN BERTRAND/SHUTTERSTOCK ©

Left Festa Major de Gràcia (p152) **Right** Imagine Dragons concert at Palau Sant Jordi **Below** Razzmatazz nightclub (p107)

DRINKS WITH A VIEW

Barcelona's rooftop bars offer stunning views; try Ayre Rosselló, Iberostar Paseo de Gracia, Hotel Colón, H10 Mimosa and Hotel Catalonia Barcelona Plaza.

LIVE MUSIC GALORE

Barcelona teems with venues hosting music for all tastes. Popular places include Palau Sant Jordi, Razzmatazz and Sala BARTS.

RIGHT: AGEFOTOSTOCK/ALAMY STOCK PHOTO ©, LEFT: BEARFOTOS/SHUTTERSTOCK ©

↑ DANCE THE NIGHT AWAY

Barcelona offers dance floors for all musical persuasions. Nightclubs usually open around midnight and many enforce a smart casual dress code (no sports shoes).

Best nightlife experiences

- **Enjoy vermouth like a local in one of Gràcia's lively squares** (p148)
- **Head to L'Eixample for a glamorous cocktail or craft beer** (p135)
- **Choose El Raval for an alternative scene with all kinds of options** (p66)
- **End the night at one of Barri Gòtic's popular nightclubs or live music venues** (p50)

ARCHITECTS' **PLAYGROUND**

Walking around Barcelona you can't help but be fascinated by the buildings around you. It sometimes feels like there's so much beauty, but too little time to appreciate every detail. Remember to walk with both eyes wide open to take in the beautiful pieces of architecture that have resulted from centuries of history and the creative genius of the city.

POL ALBARRÁN/GETTY IMAGES ©

Left Palau de la Música Catalana (p82) **Right** Carrer del Bisbe (p39), Barri Gòtic **Below** Museu Nacional d'Art de Catalunya (p177), Montjuïc

→ MEDIEVAL GEMS

Walk the old streets of Barri Gòtic and El Born, which are lined by countless examples of medieval architecture.

MODERNIST BEAUTY

L'Eixample is Barcelona's modernist district. Created in the 19th century, it was designed in a perfect grid pattern, with wide streets.

RIGHT: CORNFIELD/SHUTTERSTOCK ©, LEFT: RODRIGO GARRIDO/SHUTTERSTOCK ©

↑ CONTEMPORARY MARVELS

Old meets new in places such as MNAC (p177) near Montjuic, while contemporary architecture takes over districts such as Les Corts and Diagonal Mar.

Best architecture experiences

▸ **Marvel at the impressive cathedral and the charming little streets and squares of Barri Gòtic** (p30)

▸ **Travel back in time among Carrer de Montcada's old noble palaces** (p76)

▸ **Visit Palau de la Música Catalana not just for the music but for its magnificent modernist architecture** (p82)

▸ **Be awed by L'Eixample's chamfered corners and lesser-known buildings** (p132)

▸ **Savour one of the most memorable park walks of your life at Gaudí's Park Güell** (p146)

BEACHES & GREEN SPACES

Barcelona's architectural beauty and buzzing city life might get all the attention, but narrow medieval streets, modernist buildings and frantic crowds are not the only thing to see here. There are many more natural sights for those who would like to take a break from the city's hectic rhythm or connect with nature.

Parc del Laberint d'Horta

A romantic garden

Comprising a maze, a 14th-century country house and surrounding woodlands, this museum garden offers a peaceful atmosphere that can be hard to find in the city centre. It's one of the oldest parks in Barcelona.

Mundet

Park Güell

Gaudí's majestic garden

Planned as luxury housing but never really completed, Park Güell was later opened as a municipal garden. Marvel at the colorful mosaics or the beautiful blend of green, organic shapes and human genius.

Lesseps, Vallcarca; bus or taxi

▸ p146

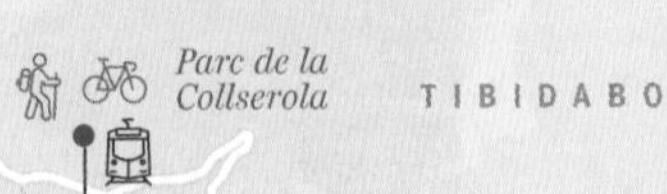

Collserola Park

World's largest metropolitan park

With 8000 hectares of protected nature, Collserola Park (pictured right) is a must for outdoor enthusiasts. Locals escape here to go hiking and cycling with splendid views of the city tucked between the mountains and the sea.

Take the Funicular de Vallvidrera

Parc de la Ciutadella

A large green oasis

An escape for those living in the city centre, the park's (pictured right) 17 hectares provide a wide space to walk, jog, enjoy a picnic or do some people-watching. Includes public buildings and museums, a small lake and an impressive fountain.

Ciutadella | Vila Olímpica, Arc de Triomf

▸ p88

Barceloneta Beach

The city's famous beach

Apart from the nice stretch of sand and sea, at Barceloneta there's always something that will keep you busy, from volleyball matches to street performers, sand castle artists and great restaurants.

Barceloneta, Vila Olímpica

▸ p92

Montjuïc

A mountain of surprises

Not exactly a mountain but rather a hill, located in the city centre between Plaça d'Espanya and the big avenue of Paral·lel, Montjuïc combines nature, culture, museums and exhibition spaces, a fortress and stunning views of the city and harbour.

Pl. Espanya, Poble Sec, Paral·lel

▸ p180

Neighbourhood celebrations take place all year round. These are some of the most popular ones:

La Mercé

Festa Major de Gràcia

Festes de Santa Eulàlia

Festa Major de Sant Antoni

Festa Major de Sants

Festa Major de la Barceloneta

MARCIN D/500PX ©

MORE THAN **SIGHTSEEING**

Take a break from museums and crossing the city's famous landmarks off your to-do list by experiencing some of these fun-packed activities. From football games to street parties, amusement parks with panoramic views to workouts in unique locations, the list of experiences to try in Barcelona is as diverse as it is endless.

Best entertainment experiences

▶ **Witness the power of football at a live match in the world-famous Camp Nou** (p160)

▶ **Visit one of Europe's oldest amusement parks and Barcelona's highest viewpoint at Tibidabo** (p159)

▶ **Be part of one of the city's biggest street parties at the Festa Major de Gràcia** (pictured; p152)

▶ **Get sporty in Montjüic, whether it's for a walk, a run, or a swim in a panoramic pool** (p180)

↘ TOP CHILD-FRIENDLY EVENTS

Tió de Nadal Meet the Catalan version of Santa Claus next to the Cathedral during the Christmas season.

Three Kings Parade The Three Kings arrive in Barcelona and parade around the city, giving out sweets.

Festes de Santa Eulàlia Traditional activities for the whole family.

MAKING FAMILY **MEMORIES**

Those visiting Barcelona with children will find no shortage of memorable, child-friendly experiences. The city is a fun place to be for both adults and children, with many museums, outdoor spaces, playgrounds, parks and shops suited to families.

Best experiences for families with children

- **Experiment with science at CosmoCaixa, a museum designed especially for children** (pictured)
- **Make a splash without leaving the city at Barceloneta beach** (p92)
- **Satisfy your sweet tooth at Barcelona's chocolate street** (p45)
- **Play kings and queens at Montjuïc Castle before picnicking in nearby gardens** (p175)
- **Step back in time among spectacular ships at the Maritime Museum** (p70)

FRANTICOO/SHUTTERSTOCK ©

HISTORY & ART IN EVERY **CORNER**

From renowned museums and exhibition spaces to street art, from art galleries to public spaces boasting pieces created by big names, there is no doubt that Barcelona is one big museum. Breathe art and history wherever you go, or follow these tips if you don't know where to start.

LEFT: ARCHER ALL SQUARE/SHUTTERSTOCK ©, BOTTOM: MARCO RUBINO/SHUTTERSTOCK ©

★ OPEN-AIR ART

Celebrated pieces open 24/7 include Picasso's friezes at the Col·legi d'Arquitectes, Joan Miró's mosaic on La Rambla and his mural at the airport, or the iconic 'The Wounded Shooting Star' in Barceloneta.

Best cultural encounters

- **Trace Barcelona's Roman and medieval splendor at MUHBA Plaça del Rei** (p49)
- **Admire the extensive Romanesque art collection at Museu Nacional d'Art de Catalunya** (p177)
- **Discover Picasso's legacy at the Picasso Museum in El Born** (p84)
- **Chase Gaudí's art around the city, from Park Güell to Gràcia, l'Eixample and El Raval** (p162)

← MUSEUMS FOR EVERYONE

Most museums offer free entry on the first Sunday of the month. Some also offer free access at certain times on specific days of the week.

Top left Park Güell (p146)
Left Picasso Museum (p84)

SHOP TILL YOU DROP

A creative city such as Barcelona has a lot more to offer than art and architecture. When it comes to shopping, whether it's for fashion, accessories, souvenirs, books or home decor, you won't have to look far to buy your own little piece of the city's beauty and character.

LEFT: ANTON_IVANOV/SHUTTERSTOCK © BOTTOM: MICHAEL HEFFERNAN/LONELY PLANET ©

★ FOODIE FINDS

Head to La Boqueria for a market experience where you'll get to see and try local delicacies. Taste a wide range of regional Catalan and Spanish quality foods and choose your favourite ones to take back home with you.

Best fashion & shopping experiences

- **Shop on the city's famous modernist boulevard, Passeig de Gràcia** (p130)
- **Hunt for unique treasures in the narrow alleys of El Born and Barri Gòtic**(p52)
- **Be nice to the planet and shop at Gràcia's many eco-friendly stores** (p144)
- **Search for vintage finds that deserve a second life in El Raval** (p71)

← FASHION MADE IN BARCELONA

Local labels include Desigual, Tous, Etnia Barcelona, Pronovias, Lola Casademunt, Custo Barcelona, Avellaneda and Eiko Ai. Discover others in the city's many concept stores and small boutiques.

Top left Passeig de Gràcia
Left El Quim de La Boqueria (p63)

Peak season

Demand for accommodation peaks during summer. Book tours, flights and insurance in advance at lonelyplanet.com/bookings.

↓ Beach days

To avoid the crowds in Barceloneta and surroundings, go between Bogatell and Llevant, or take a short train ride to Castelldefels, Badalona or Montgat.

▶ p97

→ Nit de Sant Joan

Celebrated 23 and 24 June, traditionally by making bonfires. Crowds head to the beach or stay home for a special dinner with family and friends.

↖ Music festivals

Popular summer festivals include Brunch in the Park, Festival Jardins de Pedralbes, Primavera Sound, Sónar, Cruïlla, DGTL, Circuit and Barcelona Beach Festival.

JUNE

Average daytime max: 25°C
Days of rainfall: 4

JULY

Barcelona in SUMMER

Rooftop terrace season

Between May and October, many hotel rooftops open their doors to the public to enjoy a drink or food at their bars.

↗ Festa Major de Gràcia

The Gràcia festival takes over the neighbourhood's streets with colourful installations, concerts, dances and more between 15 and 21 August.

▶ p152

↗ Festa Major de Sants

The Sants district's popular street festival takes place during August. Expect concerts, dance parties and elaborately decorated streets.

Average daytime max: 28°C
Days of rainfall: 4

AUGUST

Average daytime max: 28°C
Days of rainfall: 5

August closures

Many shops and offices, especially small shops and public offices, close for holidays during August.

Check out the full calendar of events

↘ La Diada

The National Day of Catalonia commemorates the fall of Barcelona during the Spanish war of succession with crowded streets, parades and concerts.

Festa Major de la Barceloneta

Another multiday neighbourhood festival (around 29 September), this time in Barceloneta, to celebrate its patron saint, St Michael.

La Mercè

An open-air festival lasting several days around 23 September, La Mercè is dedicated to Our Lady of Mercy, the city's patron saint. Find the full program on barcelona.cat/lamerce/en.

→ Theatre season

With autumn comes the beginning of a new theatre season in the city, which makes an ideal activity for colder and rainy days.

SEPTEMBER

Average daytime max: 24°C
Days of rainfall: 8

OCTOBER

Barcelona in AUTUMN

↘ Barcelona Jazz Festival

A well-established musical event that has been taking place every year since 1966, usually between October and November.

↓ Castanyada

A traditional festivity celebrated on 1 November for All Saints Day; typically includes roasted chestnuts and *panellets* (sweets made with almond paste and pine nuts).

48h Open House

An architecture festival taking place around the end of October, when many buildings are opened up for the public to visit and admire.

Average daytime max: 21°C
Days of rainfall: 8

NOVEMBER

Average daytime max: 16°C
Days of rainfall: 6

← Food markets

Autumn is also the high season for food and food truck markets; check out Van Van Market, Eat Gaudí and Palo Alto.

Packing notes

Bring layers for warm days and chilly evenings, and don't forget an umbrella.

↘ Christmas in Barcelona

Christmas Eve, Christmas Day and St Stephen's Day are all celebrated. Christmas markets start at the end of November, the most important being Santa Llúcia and Sagrada Família markets.

Three Kings Parade

The holiday season lasts until 6 January, when elaborate carriages and raining sweets parade across the entire city centre.

New Year's Eve

The firework display on Plaça d'Espanya is a classic. Restaurants and nightclubs organise special menus and parties (reservations are strongly recommended).

↙ Festa dels Tres Tombs

An animal parade in honour of St Anthony, the patron saint of animals. This event has been taking place in Sant Antoni since at least the early 19th century.

DECEMBER

Average daytime max: 13°C
Days of rainfall: 5

JANUARY

Barcelona in WINTER

→ Carnival

Apart from colourful parades in different neighbourhoods, Carnival celebrations include the Carnival King's arrival, masked balls and the 'burial of the sardine'.

Festa de Santa Eulàlia

Takes place for four days in Barri Gòtic; the neighbourhood is taken over by parades with giants, fire runs, *castellers* (human towers) and *sardanes* (traditional dance).

↓ Llum BCN

A festival that merges light, art, music and architecture in surprising installations all around the Poblenou district.

FEBRUARY

Average daytime max: 12°C
Days of rainfall: 5

Average daytime max: 13°C
Days of rainfall: 5

Festa de Sant Medir

Taking place in Gràcia, this festivity starts with a pilgrimage to the Ermita de Sant Medir and ends with a musical parade and raining sweets.

↘ Festa de Sant Josep Oriol

Taking place around Santa Maria del Pi, in Barri Gòtic, festivities include parades with giant figures and reenactments of the legend of the saint.

↗ Zurich Barcelona Marathon

This annual marathon attracts runners from around the world. Starting from Plaça d'Espanya, the circuit passes by some of the city's famous landmarks.

Barcelona Beer Festival

Beer enthusiasts can taste over 650 beers and attend different activities at this annual craft beer festival.

MARCH

Average daytime max: 16°C
Days of rainfall: 5

APRIL

Barcelona in SPRING

↘ Holy Week (Semana Santa)

Easter celebrations include the blessing of the palms and processions. Friday, Sunday and Monday (when the Mona de Pasqua or 'Easter cake' is eaten) are bank holidays.

Sant Jordi

Watch the city get full of roses and books on every street corner during St George's Day, which honours Catalonia's patron saint, when couples exchange gifts.

▶ p179

↗ Museum Night

Museums around the city are open for free until late at night and offer special activities, workshops, live music concerts and more.

Average daytime max: 18°C
Days of rainfall: 7

MAY

Average daytime max: 21°C
Days of rainfall: 6

← Ciutat Flamenco Festival

Barcelona hosts an annual flamenco festival, which includes a congress and live performances taking place in different venues.

MY PERFECT DAY IN **BARCELONA**

By Soledad Abella
@myplaces andstories

MEDIEVAL AND MODERNIST HIGHLIGHTS

Start the day with a coffee and an *ensaïmada* (sweet pastry) to go. Set out early to explore the quiet streets of Barri Gòtic before the crowds arrive. Bring your camera along and cycle to some of the most photogenic spots in the city, from the Cathedral and Pont del Bisbe to the picturesque little streets of El Born, the modernist masterpieces on Passeig de Gràcia and, of course, the Sagrada Família.

BEST VIEWPOINTS

Bunkers del Carmel for panoramic views.

Tibidabo, the highest spot in the city.

Park Güell for city views and Gaudí architecture.

A MOSAIC OF BITES AND SIPS

If happiness is located in your stomach, you're lucky. Start the day with a luscious brunch in Poblenou, then head to Barceloneta to whet your lunch-appetite with a *bomba* and a glass of wine or *vermut*. Since you're there, lunch on locally caught seafood. Afternoon cravings? L'Eixample boasts some of the city's most indulgent pastry shops. And if you're thirsty, check out the *barrio's* craft beer joints. For dinner, devour the neighbourhood's international food scene, washing it down with a chic cocktail, of course.

By Mireia Font
@mireiafont gastro

WHY I LOVE BARCELONA

As colourful and bright as Gaudí's ceramic-tile mosaics, Barcelona's cultural diversity is what makes me fall madly in love with the city.

Above Panoramic city views from Bunkers del Carmel **Right** Strolling the streets of El Born

BARS, LOCAL LIFE, GAUDÍ

Take things slowly with an *esmorzar de forquilla* breakfast at any eatery in Mercat del Ninot. Sated, hop on the metro towards Vallcarca to visit Parc Güell, while checking out some of the best city views. Around noon, walk to Gràcia to have *vermut* like a local in Bodega Marín, followed by strolling the alleys of multicultural El Raval, and checking the art exhibition at CCCB. Spend the evening in a local bar terrace in Sant Antoni, such as Bar Calders.

By Joan Torres
@againstthecompass

WHY I LOVE BARCELONA

I love the city's Mediterranean lifestyle, top culinary experiences and welcoming, vibrant social life, all sprinkled with doses of cosmopolitanism and staggering architecture. And all this without losing its Catalan essence!

MAZAREKIC/SHUTTERSTOCK ©

By Kyoko Kawaguchi
@KawaguchiKyoko

EXERCISE AND CHILL AFTERNOON

Work off the *pintxos* and beers from the night before by heading to Montjuïc for a morning outdoor yoga class. After a good sweat, head to Castell de Montjuïc or stroll down to Museu Nacional d'Art de Catalunya. In the afternoon, indulge in well-earned *vermut* time at Carrer del Parlament while flipping through the pages of a secondhand book bought at Mercat Dominical de Sant Antoni.

WHY I LOVE BARCELONA

The cultural diversity of Spain and its cosmopolitan atmosphere speak to me. Dancing in the traditional Sardana circle, I feel this more intensely than ever!

7 Things to Know About BARCELONA

INSIDER TIPS TO HIT THE GROUND RUNNING

1 Public transport card

Tickets can be bought at any metro station or via the TMB app. The T-Casual card is a personal card (linked to your ID) for 10 combined journeys. A supplementary payment is required for the airport's metro and train stations. The T-Dia card allows unlimited travel within 24 hours, and the Hola Barcelona Card offers two-, three-, four- and five-day options.

▶ See more about travelling around Barcelona on p208

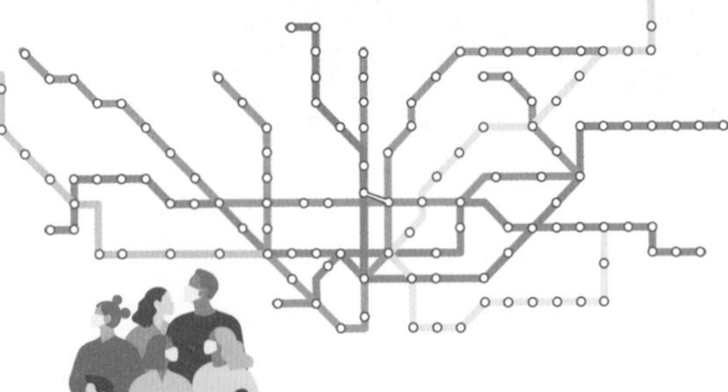

2 Shared mobility

There are many possible ways to move around Barcelona other than public transport thanks to shared mobility services. Some of the most popular ones include bike sharing apps Bolt, Donkey Bike and Movi; scooter sharing apps Yego, Scoot and eCooltra; and (stand up) electric scooter sharing apps Reby and Bird. Vehicles can be unlocked and paid for using the respective apps.

3 COVID-19

Entry requirements for Spain can be found on travelsafe.spain.info/en. Other COVID-19 regulations, including restrictions on mobility, opening times, events and social gatherings, can be checked at barcelona.cat/covid19/en.

4 Sunday closures

Many shops, including supermarkets, are usually closed on Sundays and bank holidays. An official list of exceptional opening days can be found at ajuntament.barcelona.cat/comerc/en/observatory/business-hours.

5 Catalan language and culture

Catalan is an official language in Barcelona and Catalonia, alongside Spanish. Catalan is widely spoken by the local population and public signs are either in both Spanish and Catalan or in Catalan only. Public education is taught in Catalan, and even at university level only certain courses are held in Spanish or English.

Catalonia, although it shares common elements with the rest of the country, has many of its own unique cultural traditions and festivities. Culture, language and a long history are important aspects to keep in mind when approaching Catalan politics and the region's divergences with the central Spanish government, which have led to tense episodes in recent years. The subject is very complex and requires thorough examination to be truly understood. Visitors are well advised to be aware of sensitivities here, which they will probably notice at some point during their stay.

7 Local lingo

Gràcies/Merci – Thank you

Si us plau – Please

Bon dia – Good morning

Bona tarda – Good afternoon

Bona nit – Good night

Adéu – Goodbye

Fem un café? – Used to invite someone to grab a coffee with you

Fer el vermut – 'Going for a vermouth', a local tradition on Sundays before lunch

▶ See also the Language chapter on p218

6 Museum card

The official Barcelona City Card by Turisme de Barcelona can be bought online or at any tourist information office. It is valid for 72, 96 or 120 hours and includes free access to at least 25 museums and spaces, discounts for additional sights, and free public transport including to and from the airport. The Barcelona Express Card is valid for 48 hours.

Read, Listen, Watch & Follow

READ

Cathedral of the Sea (Ildefonso Falcones; 2006) Travel back to medieval Barcelona.

Homage to Catalonia (George Orwell; 1938) The writer's memoir after fighting in the Spanish Civil War.

The Shadow of the Wind (Carlos Ruiz Zafón; 2001) A gripping mystery set in Barcelona in the early 1900s.

The City of Marvels (Eduardo Mendoza Garriga; 1986) Delve into Barcelona at the turn of the 20th century.

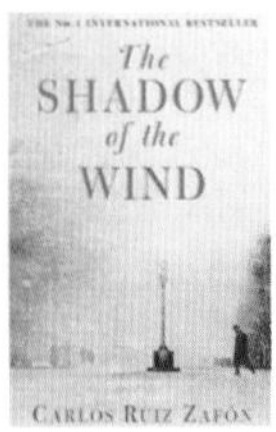

LISTEN

Qué Bonita es Barcelona (Jorge Sepúlveda; 1948) A list of reasons why Barcelona is so special, which are as valid today as they were in 1948.

Barcelona (George Ezra; 2015) A song that takes you on a dramatic, joyful short trip to Barcelona.

Rumba de Barcelona (Manu Chao; 2002) The singer's (pictured) ode to Barcelona, representing the its lively personality.

Barcelona (Freddie Mercury and Monsterrat Caballé; 1988) The official theme song for the 1992 Olympic Games.

XAVI TORRENT/GETTY IMAGES ©

Barcelona Hechicera (Peret; 1992) Inspired by rumba catalana, a rhythm born among the city's Gypsy community.

WATCH

Two Catalonias (2018) Documentary on the political conflict between Catalonia's independence movement and Spain's central government.

Vicky Cristina Barcelona (2008) Captivating city views in this Woody Allen rom-com.

Pot Luck/The Spanish Apartment (2002) Chronicles the study-abroad experience of international students in Barcelona.

All About My Mother (1999) Pedro Almodóvar's famous comedy-drama is set in Barcelona.

La Catedral del Mar (2018) Eight-part series of a serf's search for a better life in 14th-century Barcelona.

KEVIN KANE/GETTY IMAGES ©

ALLSTAR PICTURE LIBRARY LTD./ ALAMY STOCK PHOTO ©

FOLLOW

Time Out Barcelona (timeout.com/barcelona) Guide to events, restaurants and things to do.

visit Barcelona
@visitbarcelona Barcelona Tourism Board's official account.

BARCELONA SECRETA
@barcelonasecreta Sharing Barcelona's secret/not-so-secret must-sees.

Barcelona Navigator (barcelonanavigator.com) Things to do and places to stay and eat.

@barcelonafood experience Recommendations for the city's food scene.

Sate your Barcelona dreaming with a virtual vacation at lonelyplanet.com/barcelona-planning-a-trip

LA RAMBLA & BARRI GÒTIC

HISTORY | CULTURE | VIBRANT

Experience Barri Gòtic online

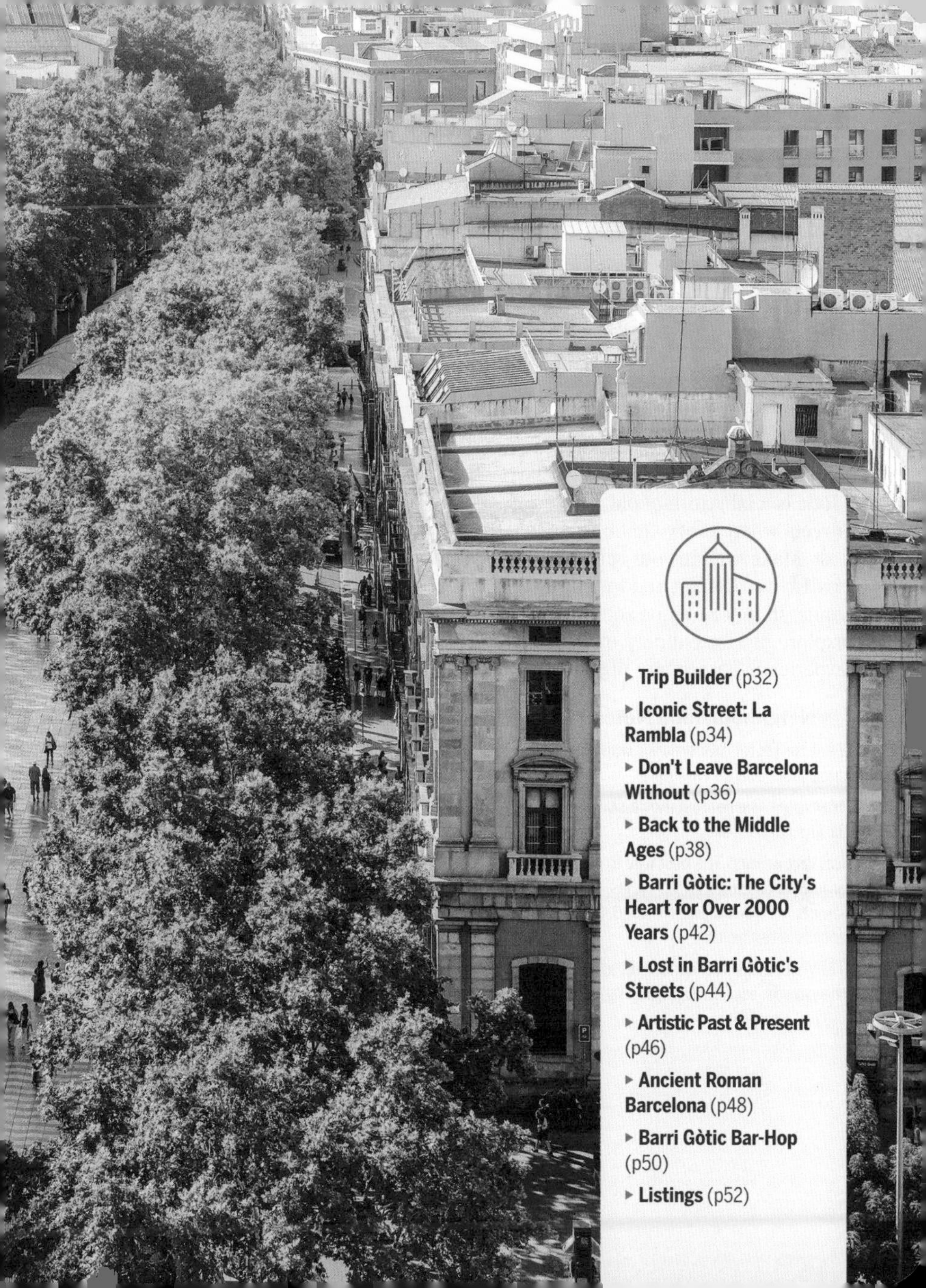

LA RAMBLA & BARRI GÒTIC
Trip Builder

TAKE YOUR PICK OF MUST-SEES AND HIDDEN GEMS

The neighbourhood that saw the birth and rise of Barcelona, Barri Gòtic is a labyrinth of old medieval streets where everyone hopes to get lost. Make time in your schedule to discover Roman and medieval gems, shop for unique souvenirs, explore diverse culinary offerings and experience Barcelona's nightlife.

Neighbourhood Notes

Best for Historic landmarks, walking, shopping, food and nightlife.

Transport The nearest metro stations are Jaume I and Liceu.

Getting around The best way to get around is on foot. Avoid bicycles, as the streets are narrow and crowded. Car access is restricted.

Tip Visit earlier in the morning to avoid the crowds, especially during high season.

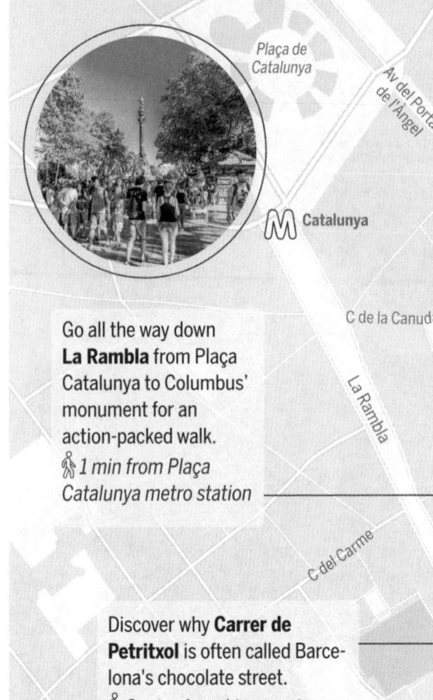

Go all the way down **La Rambla** from Plaça Catalunya to Columbus' monument for an action-packed walk.
1 min from Plaça Catalunya metro station

Discover why **Carrer de Petritxol** is often called Barcelona's chocolate street.
3 mins from Liceu metro station

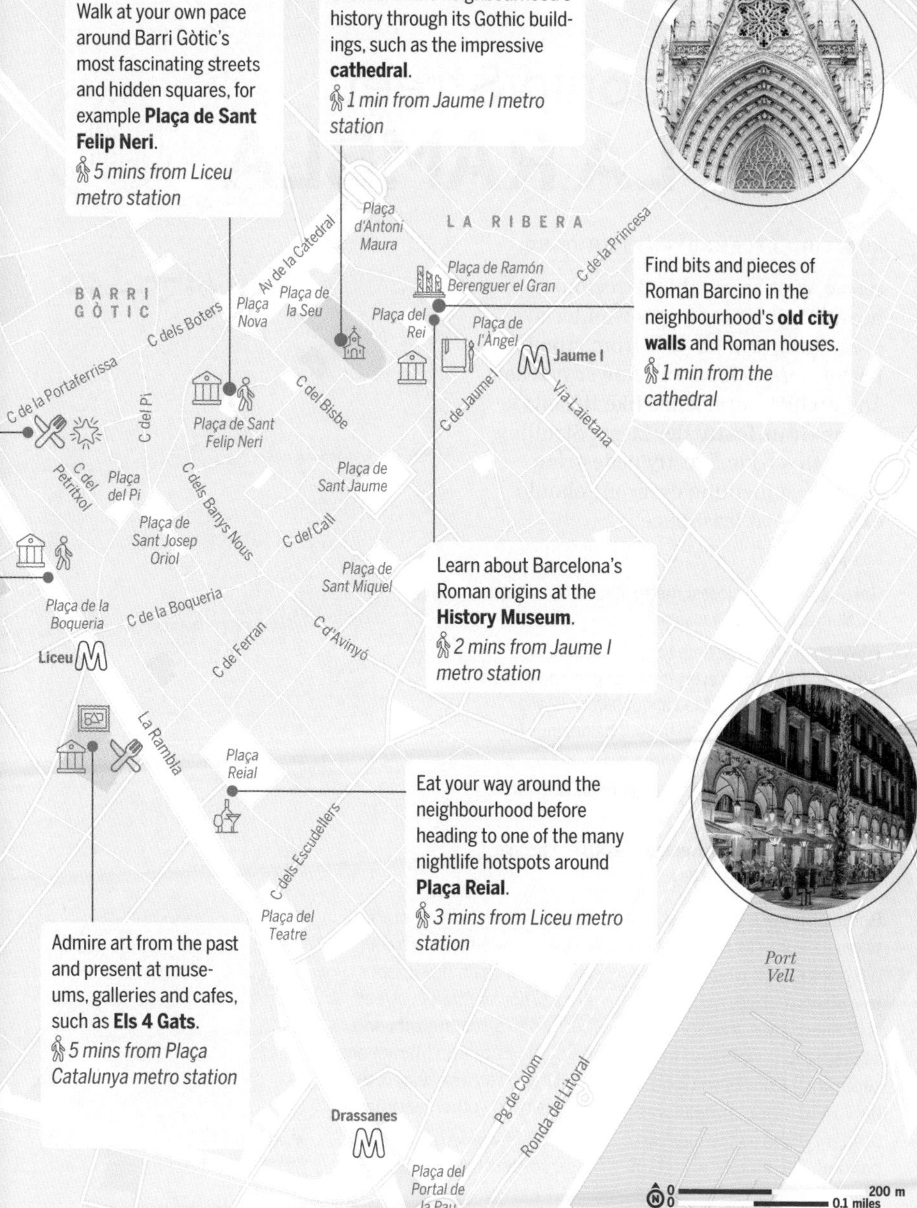

Walk at your own pace around Barri Gòtic's most fascinating streets and hidden squares, for example **Plaça de Sant Felip Neri**.
5 mins from Liceu metro station
Breathe in the neighbourhood's history through its Gothic buildings, such as the impressive **cathedral**.
1 min from Jaume I metro station
Find bits and pieces of Roman Barcino in the neighbourhood's **old city walls** and Roman houses.
1 min from the cathedral
Learn about Barcelona's Roman origins at the **History Museum**.
2 mins from Jaume I metro station
Eat your way around the neighbourhood before heading to one of the many nightlife hotspots around **Plaça Reial**.
3 mins from Liceu metro station
Admire art from the past and present at museums, galleries and cafes, such as **Els 4 Gats**.
5 mins from Plaça Catalunya metro station
LA RIBERA
BARRI GÒTIC
Plaça d'Antoni Maura
Av de la Catedral
Plaça de Ramón Berenguer el Gran
C de la Princesa
Plaça Nova
Plaça de la Seu
Plaça del Rei
Plaça de l'Àngel
Jaume I
C dels Boters
C de la Portaferrissa
C del Pi
Plaça de Sant Felip Neri
C del Bisbe
C de Jaume I
Via Laietana
C del Petritxol
Plaça del Pi
C dels Banys Nous
Plaça de Sant Jaume
Plaça de Sant Josep Oriol
C del Call
Plaça de Sant Miquel
Plaça de la Boqueria
C de la Boqueria
C de Ferran
C d'Avinyó
Liceu
La Rambla
Plaça Reial
C dels Escudellers
Plaça del Teatre
Port Vell
Drassanes
Pg de Colom
Ronda del Litoral
Plaça del Portal de la Pau
0 200 m
0 0.1 miles

01 Iconic Street: LA RAMBLA

BUSTLING | FLAMBOYANT | AMUSING

Walk down this Barcelona beauty and let your eyes wander over everything around you, from street performers to food and flower markets, and architectural gems like the city's iconic Gran Teatre del Liceu. Strolling down this wide, mostly pedestrian street is something everyone should experience at least once.

How to

Getting here The closest metro stations are Plaça Catalunya, Liceu or Drassanes.

When to go The best time to see La Rambla is during the day, when everything is open and there's no reason to be concerned about safety. In any case, always pay attention to your belongings to avoid pickpocketing incidents.

Need to know La Rambla can get really busy, so be prepared and patient.

Fun tip Pre-COVID, an average of 200,000 people visited La Rambla each day.

Barcelona's busiest street takes its name from the Arabic word *ramla,* which refers to a stream where rainwater is drained – and the city's sewage too. A wall used to separate it from Barri Gòtic until 1440, when the wall was brought down as the city expanded. The stream was then diverted and it slowly started to become the lively street it is today, with its newspaper kiosks, flower stands, street performers, restaurants and bars, the Boquería Market and the Gran Teatre del Liceu, as well as many other landmarks.

Spot this piece of art that everyone steps on Artist

Above right Mosaic by Joan Miró
Right Gran Teatre del Liceu

HERACLES KRITIKOS/SHUTTERSTOCK ©

FRIMUFILMS/SHUTTERSTOCK ©

Joan Miró left his mark right on La Rambla. Look for his colourful circular mosaic on the ground in the middle of the pedestrian area.

Celebrate Barcelona Football Club's victories Font de Canaletas is not just a fountain – it's the place where the city's football club supporters gather to celebrate their victories.

Experience the old charm of the city's opera house Buy a ticket for a show at the Gran Teatre del Liceu so you can appreciate the beauty of the building and also enjoy it the way it was meant to be enjoyed.

Go all the way to the top of the Columbus monument You'll be rewarded by impressive panoramic views of the city and the sea. Located at the end of La Rambla, this popular landmark is 60m high – but don't worry, there's an elevator.

Watch a live flamenco show Although it's traditionally from the south of Spain, if you want to experience a flamenco show head to Tablao Flamenco Cordobés, where you can choose between a dinner and show or a drink and show option.

Don't Leave Barcelona **WITHOUT**

01

04

05

02

08

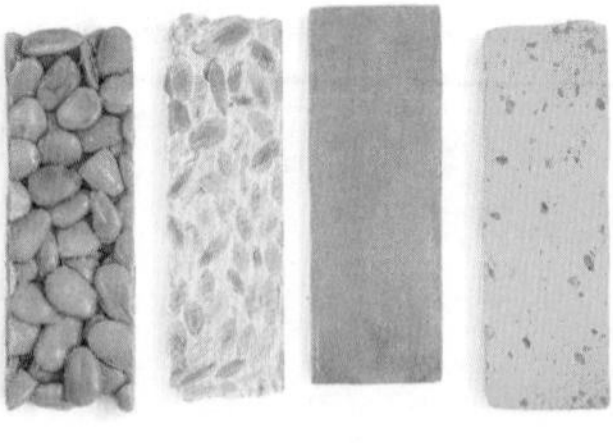

01 Espardenyes

These traditional espadrilles are made with hemp, jute and fabric. If you want to give shoemaking a try, you can join a workshop and make them yourself!

02 Cava

Catalonia's famous sparkling wine is usually *barcelonins'* preferred drink for celebrations and special occasions, but not only.

03 Salsa Espinaler

This tiny bottle is a classic at any *vermut* (aperitif). It's made with vinegar, paprika, black pepper and other spices and it's normally eaten with chips, olives and preserved foods.

04 Porró

A wine pitcher made of glass that was invented in Catalonia and makes wine drinking (and sharing) easier.

05 Caganer

A small human figure (often a famous person) in a defecating position, the *caganer* always catches the attention of first-time visitors. It can be found at most souvenir shops.

06 Barcelona Football Club merchandise
Fans will enjoy visiting one of the FC Barcelona official stores and buying an official product, from T-shirts to scarves and small accessories.

07 Sangria Lolea
Not just great-tasting sangria, but also beautiful-looking bottles. Five versions can be bought at Casa Lolea as well as some liquor stores and supermarkets.

08 Turrón
Nougat made of honey, sugar, egg whites and almonds. Some of the best places to buy turrón are Planelles Donat, La Campana and Torrons Vicens.

09 Spices
An important part of local cuisine, take home some spices such as smoked paprika and saffron to recreate the best dishes you tried in Barcelona.

02 Back to the MIDDLE AGES

MEDIEVAL | GOTHIC | FASCINATING

Explore the city's oldest neighbourhood, whose history spans over 2000 years. Founded by the Romans, it was during the Middle Ages that Barcelona's importance grew and it became a centre for politics and trade. Spend time understanding the city's glorious medieval years and soaking in its architectural beauty.

KAVALENKAVAVOLHA/GETTY IMAGES ©

How to

Getting here The nearest metro station is Jaume I.

Getting around Barri Gòtic is best explored on foot due to the narrow streets and pedestrian areas.

When to visit It's a great place to visit at any time of the day, but mornings are best for those looking to avoid crowds.

Tip When visiting the Cathedral make sure you walk around the surrounding streets too, for more Gothic sights, museums and other notable buildings.

PACO FREIRE/SOPA IMAGES/GETTY IMAGES ©

Visit Barri Gòtic's Cathedral, Its Most Impressive Building

In a neighbourhood where streets are narrow and houses were made to be crammed, the **Cathedral of the Holy Cross and Saint Eulalia** stands out with its imposing size and the wide square in front of it.

The cathedral was built between the 13th and the 15th centuries, but a big part of the facade and the central tower were actually added much later on, between the late 19th and early 20th century. Make sure to visit the courtyard, which is home to 13 geese. It is also possible to take an elevator up to the roof, where you can get up close to the towers and enjoy the panoramic views.

TOMASSEREDA/GETTY IMAGES ©

Top Photo Stops

Cathedral: especially the facade and the rooftop views.

Carrer del Bisbe: a narrow street with a theatrical neo-Gothic bridge.

The World Begins with Every Kiss: mural art made using 6000 images.

Plaça Reial: palm trees, porticoes and a central fountain make the perfect backdrop.

Top left Carrer del Bisbe **Left** Cathedral of the Holy Cross and Saint Eulalia **Above** A couple kiss at *The World Begins with Every Kiss* mural by artists Joan Fontcuberta and Toni Cumella

A Mysterious Street Called Carrer d'Estruc

Take a quick detour and discover this alley where it is said magicians used to live in the Middle Ages. It offers an interesting glimpse into the role of magic and healers in medieval times.

During the 14th century the street became home to a famous healer who lived and received clients here. Back then this part of the city was outside the city walls. Today the street's walls feature plaques written in Hebrew which contain talismans – legend has it that, if you read them until the end, you'll be blessed with good luck.

Rediscover the History of Barcelona's Jewish Community

The Jewish community was an important part of the city's population and lived here until 1391, when they were forced to convert or leave. They played an important role in the city's trading activities, as Christians were not

Tour Guide's Top 3

Plaça del Rei The palace of Barcelona's counts, built mostly in Gothic style. Today the buildings surrounding the square are part of Barcelona's History Museum (MUHBA). Some Roman ruins lie underneath the square.

Temple of Augustus Hidden in the corner of Carrer del Paradís you can find four preserved columns from an ancient Roman temple dedicated to the emperor Augustus, built in the 1st century BCE.

Plaça de Sant Felip Neri On the facade of the church of Sant Felip Neri it is easy to recognise shrapnel marks from a bomb dropped by the Italian air force during the Spanish Civil War.

Recommended by Ariadna Muñoz. *Ariadna is a tour guide at Ariadna Guided Tours. @ariadna_barcelona_tourguide; ariadnaguided tours.com.*

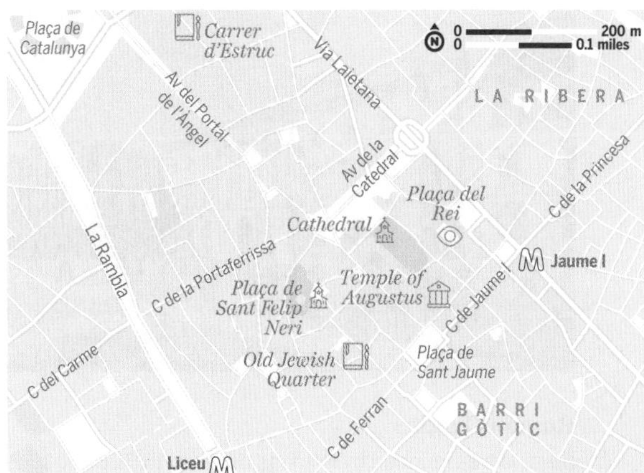

Left Temple of Augustus
Below Plaça del Rei

allowed to engage in lending money and credits in exchange for interest.

Part of Barcelona's history museum, **MUHBA El Call**, is located in the heart of the old Jewish quarter and is a museum that promotes the heritage of the city's old Jewish community. Only a minute away from El Call is an **ancient synagogue**, discovered quite recently, which is one of Europe's oldest.

Gothic Revival & 20th-Century Retouches

A good number of buildings in Barri Gòtic were renovated following the Gothic revival style between the late 19th and the 20th century, as was the case with the Cathedral.

When the city walls were torn down to expand the city, and the works to construct Via Laietana began, it was decided, after some debate, that the area would be restored according to its medieval roots. Some of the neighbourhood's iconic houses had to be placed elsewhere stone by stone, and some of the elements found in fallen buildings were added to new ones. Spot the results of this vital makeover in buildings such as the **Cathedral** itself, **Pont del Bisbe** and the **Reial Cercle Artístic**.

Barri Gòtic: The City's Heart for Over 2000 Years

Barri Gòtic was born in Roman times, boomed in the Middle Ages, and is loved today. It's not just home to century-old streets and buildings, it's a living testament to Barcelona's history and spirit, from its birth and its medieval splendour all the way through to the 21st century.

Left Plaça de Sant Jaume
Middle Plaça del Rei by night
Right Roman aqueduct ruin, Plaça Nova

JAN KRANENDONK / SHUTTERSTOCK ©

Roman Origins

Barcino was founded by Romans between 15 BCE and 10 BCE. They chose to build their settlement here due to its natural port. The centre of the old Roman city was located in what is today's Plaça de Sant Jaume. A proof that Barri Gòtic has been and remains Barcelona's governmental and religious centre is the fact that even today, in this exact spot, we can find the buildings of Palau de la Generalitat de Catalunya (the seat of the Catalan regional government), Barcelona's City Council and the Cathedral nearby.

The very first city walls were 1.5km long and had four doors. Old Barcino had governmental buildings, public baths, a temple, a necropolis and aqueducts. Remains of some of these buildings can still be seen today.

Middle Ages

Medieval times seem to come back to life when you walk these streets. It was during the Middle Ages that Barcelona became a relevant political player. Known as Ciutat Comtal, or 'city of counts', Barcelona grew thanks to the development of trade, leading to the establishment of the Maritime Consulate in 1258.

As the city expanded new walls were built, as was the port, the Royal Shipyards, the Llotja (stock exchange) and the cathedral, as well as many other churches, convents, and palaces for wealthy families.

Barcelona Expands

Barcelona's expansion outside the Barri Gòtic happened much later than you might think. It was only in 1860 when a plan for the city's expansion was presented, called Pla

Cerdà. By then the old city had become overpopulated and unsanitary, with no sewerage system or running water.

The expansion plan brought on the destruction of the city walls, the creation of a completely new district called L'Eixample and the construction of Via Laietana, an avenue that connects the harbour and the old city with the newer L'Eixample. The creation of this avenue meant the destruction of 2199 houses, affecting around 10,000 people. While many iconic buildings were irreparably lost, on a positive side, other Roman and medieval constructions were rediscovered and saved from oblivion.

> Medieval times seem to come back to life when you walk these streets.

It's also good to note that during this time parts of the Barri Gòtic were restored. Buildings were not only restored to the way they originally looked, but in some cases more neo-Gothic features were added. The most surprising of these transformations is, undoubtedly, the cathedral's facade.

Barri Gòtic Today

Today the neighbourhood is a great place to get an insight into Barcelona's past, but that's not all. Barri Gòtic has evolved with time and a visit here transmits the vibrant and modern personality of the city through its shops, restaurants, galleries, street performances and people. Visitors and locals alike come together in Barri Gòtic, the latter mostly during the afternoon and evening hours for shopping, dining, drinking and clubbing.

Must-Visits for Barcelona History

Barcelona History Museum (MUHBA) at Plaça del Rei The Roman level offers a display of villas and other buildings before continuing to the medieval section. The museum is located in three notable medieval buildings: the Plaça del Rei, the Santa Àgata chapel and Casa Padellàs.

Cathedral of the Holy Cross and Saint Eulalia Apart from visiting the inside and the cloister, it's also possible to take the elevator up to the roof.

Plaça de Sant Jaume Once the city's Roman forum, since the Middle Ages it's been home to the seat of the Catalan Government and the City Hall.

03 Lost in Barri Gòtic's STREETS

LAID-BACK | WALKING | EXPLORING

Ditch the map and let your curiosity guide you through Barcelona's oldest streets. Discover less busy but equally beautiful squares. Shop for authentic items at local boutiques and concept stores, or head to the high street for the world's most popular brands. When you're feeling hungry, you'll find all kinds of chocolates, sweets and churros along the mouth-watering 'chocolate street'.

ALESSIO CATELLI/ SHUTTERSTOCK ©

How to

Getting there Closest metro stations are Liceu, Jaume I and Plaça Catalunya.

Best time to go Go during the day to see Barri Gòtic in full light. Shops usually open at 10am and close between 7pm and 10pm. Some smaller shops may close for lunch between 1pm and 4pm.

Great starting points Plaça Reial, Plaça del Pi, Reial Cercle Artístic de Barcelona.

Fun tip During Corpus Christi look for 'dancing eggs' in the courtyards of Casa de l'Ardiaca and the Cathedral.

ANDREI BORTNIKAU / SHUTTERSTOCK ©

Left Building façade on Plaça del Pi
Bottom left 'Dancing eggs' at Casa de l'Ardiaca during Corpus Christi

Street names that tell the city's story If you pay attention to many street-name plaques, you get a picture of what that street might have looked like in the Middle Ages. One interesting name is that of **Carrer d'Espolsa-sacs**, literally the 'bag-throwing street', where monks from a convent nearby used to throw away their old vests, which looked a lot like bags. Other bits of Barcelona's medieval past are revealed in streets such as **Carrer de la Tapineria**, where workshops making a special type of shoes called tapines used to be located, and **Carrer dels Banys Nous** ('street of the new baths'), once home to the city's Jewish baths.

Barcelona's chocolate street This street's relationship with chocolate dates back to the 17th century, when different chocolate workshops opened here on **Carrer de Petritxol**. Indulge in some churros and hot chocolate at **La Pallaresa** and **Granja Dulcinea**, buy some traditional *torró* (nougat) at **Torrons Vicens** or choose chocolates to take home at **Petritxol Cocoa**.

Food, art and collectors' markets If you're looking for open-air markets in Barri Gòtic, check out **Fira del Col·lectiu d'Artesans de l'Alimentació** (artisan food market on Plaça del Pi), **Pintors del Pi** (painters' market on Plaça del Pi every Saturday and Sunday) and the **Coin and Stamp Market** on Plaça Reial (every Sunday).

Other shopping hotspots Try **Carrer de la Palla** for antiques, **Portal de l'Àngel** and **Carrer de la Portaferrissa** for high-street fashion. Smaller boutiques and concept stores are spread all around the neighbourhood and that's where you'll find the most unique pieces by local designers and artists – a great example is **La Nostra Ciutat**.

Quiet, Charming Squares

Plaça de Sant Felip Neri A fountain in the middle provides the backdrop for the quiet atmosphere here, sometimes accompanied by live music by street performers. The facade of the baroque church shows the signs of a bombing attack perpetrated by fascist planes in 1938, during the Spanish Civil War.

Plaça del Pi Sit at the terrace of Bar del Pi and admire the church of Santa Maria del Pi and the colourful buildings surrounding the square, or let time pass by while you're people-watching.

Plaça de Sant Just After you've taken your time to study the Basilica dels Sants Màrtirs Just i Pastor, take a seat and order a tapa at Cafè de l'Academia.

Plaça de la Mercè Features the beautiful Neptune Fountain and the Basilica of Our Lady of Mercy, one of Barcelona's patron saints together with Saint Eulalia.

04 Artistic Past & PRESENT

ART | HISTORY | PICASSO

Whether you're looking for art made by local artists or to soak up the city's creative atmosphere, you won't be disappointed by the options in Barri Gòtic. Visit a cafe that was the meeting point for modernist artists, follow Picasso's steps around the neighbourhood, hunt for gems in art galleries of all kinds and meet local painters at an open-air art market.

PIO3/SHUTTERSTOCK ©

How to

Getting here The closest metro stations are Plaça Catalunya, Liceu, Jaume I and Urquinaona.

When to visit During the day, when museums, exhibition spaces and markets are open.

Listings You can find a complete calendar of temporary art exhibitions on TimeOut and the city council's official website.

Tip For a full immersion into Picasso head to the Picasso Museum in El Born.

BEARFOTOS / SHUTTERSTOCK ©

Have a Drink at One of Picasso & Gaudí's Favourite Cafes

Founded in 1897, **Els 4 Gats** quickly became a classic among bohemian modernist artists. The smaller room was used as a cafe, while the bigger room hosted exhibitions and shows. Even Picasso did his very first public exhibition here.

Visit Picasso's Art School

The **Escola de la Llotja**, on Plaça de la Veronica, is a small yet impressive neoclassical building. It's no longer in use, but it's worth passing by and picturing what the young artist's life could have looked like over 120 years ago. One of the side streets, Carrer d'Avinyó, can be found in the name of his painting *Les Demoiselles d'Avignon,* which depicts female prostitutes from a brothel located on this street.

Explore Art Museums & Galleries

At **Museu Frederic Marès**, founded by the sculptor himself, the pieces date from pre-Roman times to the present day, with a big emphasis on medieval Christian sculptures. **Reial Cercle Artístic** hosts exhibitions, book presentations, conferences and concerts.

When it comes to art galleries, some popular names include **Sala Parés** (Spain's oldest art gallery, with three different exhibition spaces), **Villa del Arte** (contemporary art exhibitions), **Barcel-one** (where you can find paintings and drawings by artists such as Miró, Dalí or Picasso) and **Base Elements Art Gallery** (a street-art gallery, workshop and studio).

Left Museu Picasso, El Born
Bottom left Els 4 Gats

Open-Air Painters Market

The **Mostra d'Art Pintors del Pi** market has been taking place for over 40 years now, after a small group of artists decided to bring their paintings to the street, and to the public. Today dozens of artists exhibit their work every Saturday and Sunday on Plaça Sant Josep Oriol, with the Gothic church of Santa Maria del Pi as a backdrop. You can meet and speak to the painters themselves about their work, which ranges in style and techniques, although the majority of works are created using oil paintings and watercolours.

05 Ancient Roman BARCELONA

HISTORY | ROMAN RUINS | MUSEUMS

The splendour of medieval Barcelona is evident all around Barri Gòtic, but if you pay close attention – and you know where to look for it – you'll find the oldest foundations of the city that date back over 2000 years. Let the remains of the old Roman wall, an underground Roman quarter, an ancient Roman house, a burial ground and thermal baths paint a picture of what Roman Barcino looked like.

ANSHARPHOTO/SHUTTERSTOCK ©

How to

Getting there The closest metro stations are Jaume I and Liceu.

When to go At the time of writing, Tuesday was the only day when all four of these monuments were open to the public.

Cost The entrance fee is either free of charge, €2 or €7, depending on the monument.

Tip Some of these monuments may have reduced opening times, so it's best to check and book in advance if possible.

TOMASZ WOZNIAK/SHUTTERSTOCK ©

Left Roman gate, near Plaça Nova
Bottom left Casa Padellàs

Uncover the Roman Wall

While it is estimated that around two thirds of the wall is still lying underground, parts of the old Roman wall can be seen today in different locations. One of them is **Portal del Bisbe**, called Porta Praetoria in Roman times, the only one of four Roman doors that has been preserved. On **Plaça de Ramón Berenguer el Gran** a relatively big portion of the wall can be seen. It's interesting to notice the Roman construction at the bottom, on top of which a medieval wall was later built.

Underground at the MUHBA Plaça del Rei

Starting with an underground itinerary along the streets of a Roman quarter in ancient Barcino, the visit continues to a smaller medieval section as well as temporary modern and contemporary exhibitions. The museum also comprises the **Royal Palace** (Palau Reial Major), the **palatine chapel** and **Casa Padellàs**, a Gothic palace.

Burial Grounds at MUHBA Via Sepulcral Romana

This Roman **burial ground** was located outside the city walls, which was the tradition back then. The cemetery was discovered in the 1950s, when a square was built to replace the buildings that had been damaged during the Spanish Civil War.

Roman paintings at MUHBA Domus de Avinyó

This **Roman house** was inhabited by important Roman citizens and features wall and ceiling paintings that have been preserved quite well. At the time of writing, visits were only possible by guided group tour with advance reservation.

Barcino in Roman Times

Roman Barcelona, or Barcino, was founded in the 1st century BCE during Augustus' reign and experienced the height of its time during the 1st and 3rd centuries CE. The name 'Barcino' is said to be a Roman version of the Iberian name 'Barkeno'.

A big reason for the establishment of the colony here was the natural port, and the place chosen for the very first settlements was Mt Taber, a 16.9m-tall hill. Barcino grew to a size of between 3500 and 5000 inhabitants and the main economic activity was agriculture, especially viticulture, as well as fishing.

06 Barri Gòtic BAR-HOP

TAPAS | DRINKS | LATE NIGHT

In a city known for its nightlife, Barri Gòtic is a top spot for visitors and locals alike to gather around a table over tapas, treat themselves to a high-end gourmet meal, engage in long conversations at a wine or cocktail bar and dance the night away at one of the neighbourhood's nightclubs and live music venues.

BEARFOTOS/SHUTTERSTOCK ©

How To

When to go Many nightclubs and concert halls are open most days of the week. Weekends offer the biggest choice and the most festive atmosphere.

Late nights Barcelona's nightlife starts late. Nightclubs usually open around midnight, with most partygoers arriving between 2am and 3am.

Covid changes Opening times have changed multiple times due to COVID-19, so it's best to double-check beforehand.

Foodies' Favourites

Bodega La Palma (€) You can't leave Barcelona before having a vermouth and some tapas at this authentic and familiar bodega.

Bistro Levante (€€) Great for brunch with dishes from the Middle East.

Capet (€€€) Traditional Catalan food with a modern touch and honest flavours. A mandatory visit for the most sophisticated palates.

Recommended by Stefania Talento & Andreu Font, *foodies and Instagrammers. @inandoutbarcelona*

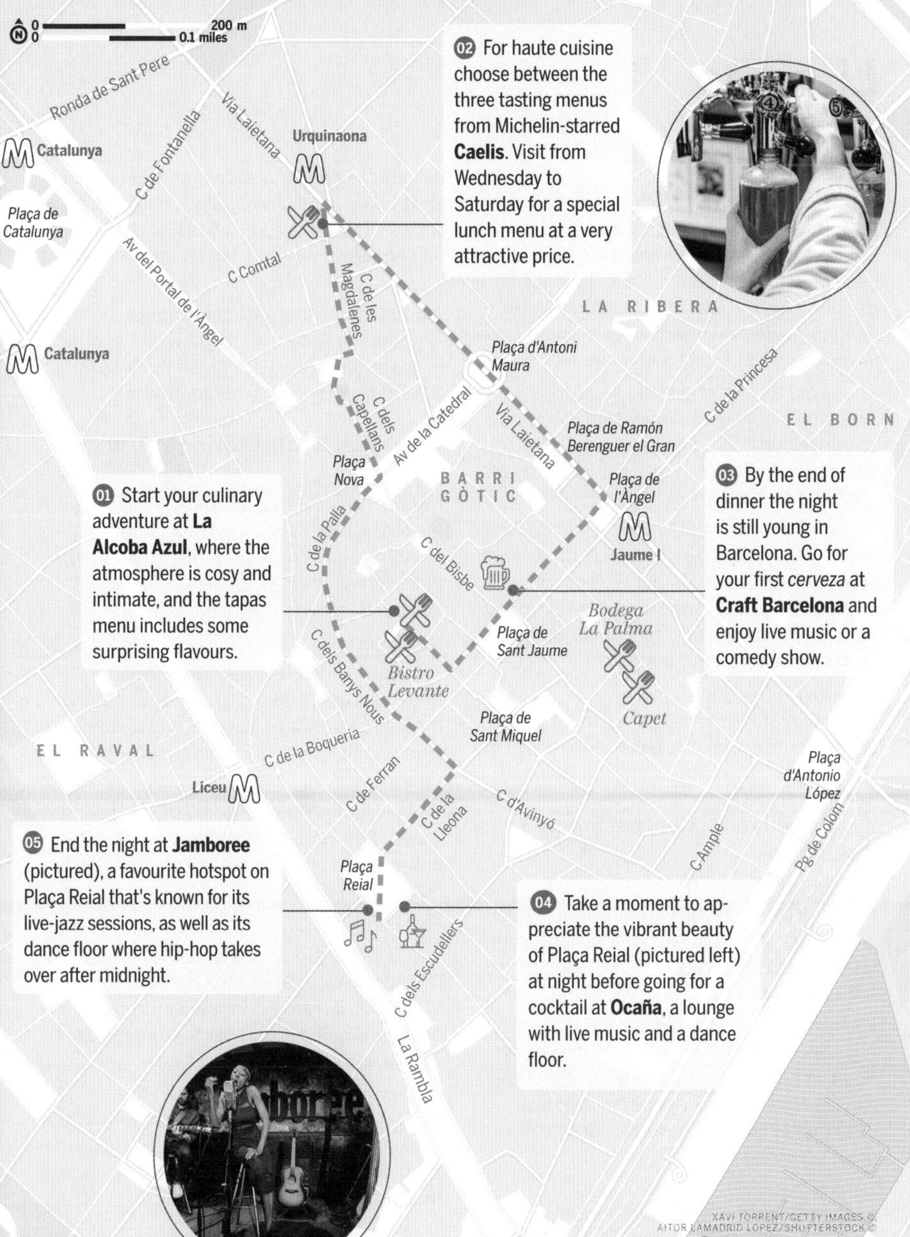

01 Start your culinary adventure at **La Alcoba Azul**, where the atmosphere is cosy and intimate, and the tapas menu includes some surprising flavours.

02 For haute cuisine choose between the three tasting menus from Michelin-starred **Caelis**. Visit from Wednesday to Saturday for a special lunch menu at a very attractive price.

03 By the end of dinner the night is still young in Barcelona. Go for your first *cerveza* at **Craft Barcelona** and enjoy live music or a comedy show.

04 Take a moment to appreciate the vibrant beauty of Plaça Reial (pictured left) at night before going for a cocktail at **Ocaña**, a lounge with live music and a dance floor.

05 End the night at **Jamboree** (pictured), a favourite hotspot on Plaça Reial that's known for its live-jazz sessions, as well as its dance floor where hip-hop takes over after midnight.

Listings

BEST OF THE REST

History & Culture

Palau Moja: Catalan Heritage House

Built in the 18th century, Palau Moja is a space dedicated to promoting Catalan heritage. Its exhibition space, shop and restaurant are open to visitors who want to learn about Catalan history, food, crafts and more.

The World Begins With Every Kiss Mural

This 8m x 3.8m mural, located on Plaça d'Isidre Nonell, was designed by Joan Fontcuberta using 6000 images submitted by the public.

MUHBA Porta de Mar i les Termes Portuàries

Literally translated as 'the door of the sea and the dockside thermal baths', this space used to be located 150m away from the sea and features part of the original Roman wall and remains of old thermal baths.

MUHBA Domus Sant Honorat

An old Roman home dating back to the 4th century, which very probably belonged to one of the city's wealthiest families during Roman times.

Handicrafts, Concept Stores & Boutiques

Sombrerería Obach

Almost 100 years old, this emblematic shop is the place to look for all types of hats, from fedoras to caps, berets, beach hats and panama hats.

La Manual Alpargatera

A traditional workshop selling an impressive range of handmade espadrilles, from classic models to more original ones in different colours and fabrics. These espadrilles make a great present or souvenir.

Cereria Subirà

Even if only for its elegant interior, which includes a beautiful staircase and statues, this shop is well worth visiting. It's the oldest candle shop in Barcelona, founded in 1761, and sells an impressive variety of handmade candles.

L'Arca

A curated selection of vintage dresses, kimonos, designer handbags, veils and other bridal accessories. Kate Winslet's dress for the *Titanic* movie was designed here.

Tapas, Haute Cuisine & Brunch

Brugarol Barcelona €€€

Creative tapas with a Japanese twist, Brugarol is a small, industrial-styled restaurant. The tasting menu includes nine dishes that combine ingredients from the land and the sea. Reservations recommended.

Koy Shunka €€€

This Michelin-starred restaurant's name translates as 'intense seasonal aromas' and the Japanese dishes, flavours and textures are outstanding. Reservations recommended.

Informal €€€

This elegant restaurant offers breath-taking views of the harbour. Located on the rooftop of the Serras Hotel, it serves colourful, modern Catalan dishes.

Milk Bar & Bistro €€

Milk Bar & Bistro claims to be the first restaurant to have introduced the concept of brunch to Barcelona. Famous for classic brunch dishes including eggs, bagels, smoothies and pancakes.

La Cereria €€

A vegetarian and vegan restaurant with a bohemian ambience. It's located in an old candle shop, which can be seen from the original sign that's still over the entrance door.

Rooftop Bars, Speakeasies & Friendly Cocktail Bars

Hotel Colón Rooftop Terrace €€
This terrace offers stunning views of the cathedral located across the plaza. The drinks and the atmosphere are nothing special, but the views are some of the best in the city.

Pipa Club €€
Ring the bell to access this 'secret' speakeasy, hidden on the 2nd floor (principal) of the building located at Plaça Reial 3. Carefully crafted cocktails in a Sherlock Holmes–inspired apartment.

Ohla Barcelona Rooftop Bar €€
Panoramic rooftop terrace featuring a pool and stylish decor, this bar is located on the top floor of Ohla Barcelona Hotel and overlooks the old city and the Montjuïc hill.

Espit Chupitos €
With three locations across Barcelona, Espit Chupitos serves over 100 types of shots. Fun atmosphere, original presentation and an endless choice.

First Cocktail Bar €
This bar's walls are covered in post-its with messages left by customers from around the world, which adds to the fun vibe. Live music, good cocktails and reasonable prices.

Bakeries & Sweet Bites

Xurreria Banys Nous €
Repeatedly proclaimed the best churros shop in Barcelona, the churros don't disappoint and vary from the classic version to those covered in chocolate or filled with cream, chocolate or Nutella.

Caelum €
A charming bakery with exposed brick walls belonging to the old public baths, which can be found in the basement. The cakes, pastries and other sweets at Caelum are made mostly by nuns and monks.

1000 WORDS/SHUTTERSTOCK©

Hotel Colón Rooftop Terrace

Planelles Donat €
In business since 1850, this neighbourhood classic sells artisan *torró* (nougats), *orxata* (vegetable milk made with ground chufa nuts) and ice cream.

Pastisseria La Colmena €
This cake shop dates back to 1849 and is heaven for those with a sweet tooth. Cakes, pastries, desserts, and a long list of sweet treats are made according to original recipes.

Live Music & Dancing

Harlem Jazz Club
A Barcelona nightlife icon and one of the city's oldest live-music venues, which hosts different genres, but especially jazz, blues and soul, almost daily.

El Bombón Salsa
Although quite small, El Bombón is loved by salsa fans and offers the ideal atmosphere to show off your salsa, bachata, merengue and other Latin dance moves.

Nevermind
With its indoor skating bowl, this bar is paradise for the many skaters you'll see in Barcelona. A second location can be found in El Raval.

Scan to find more things to do in Barri Gòtic online

EL RAVAL

DIVERSE | YOUNG | ALTERNATIVE

Experience El Raval online

EL RAVAL
Trip Builder

TAKE YOUR PICK OF MUST-SEES AND HIDDEN GEMS

El Raval has a strong and distinct personality that makes it stand out from all other neighbourhoods in Barcelona. Experience the alternative heartbeat of this melting pot through its street art, contemporary-art museums, bits and pieces of history and its food and nightlife – a mix of old school, multicultural and trendy spots.

Neighbourhood Notes

Best for Barcelona's famous food market, street art, bar-hopping and unique vintage finds.

Transport The nearest metro stations are Universitat, Liceu, Drassanes, Paral·lel and Sant Antoni.

Getting around It is best to get around El Raval on foot.

Tips The higher crime rate than in other areas shouldn't be a reason to avoid El Raval, but it should be a warning that extra caution is necessary.

Take a deep dive into contemporary art at **Barcelona Contemporary Art Museum (MACBA)** or one of the neighbourhood's contemporary art centres.
5 mins from Universitat metro station

Chase street art all around the area, which can feel like an open-air gallery at times, such as in **Carrer de l'Aurora**.
2 mins from Rambla del Raval

Explore the neighbourhood's medieval past in places like **Sant Pau del Camp**.
5 mins from Drassanes metro station

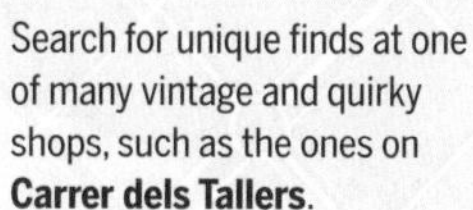

Search for unique finds at one of many vintage and quirky shops, such as the ones on **Carrer dels Tallers**.
3 mins from Plaça Catalunya metro station

Visit one of Europe's largest food markets, **La Boqueria**, and see, smell and taste local cuisine.
1 min from Liceu metro station

Sit down at **Jardins de Rubió i Lluch**, a peaceful oasis, and let the scenes around you tell you about El Raval's history, personality and people.
5 mins from Liceu metro station

Admire Gaudí's first commission, **Palau Güell**, to understand how the genius' style evolved over time.
1 min from La Rambla

Explore El Raval's diversity through its flavours. A good place to start is **Rambla del Raval**.
5 mins from Liceu or Paral·lel metro station

Plaça de Catalunya
Catalunya
C de Pelai
C dels Tallers
La Rambla
C de Valldonzella
Plaça dels Àngels
C de Joaquín Costa
BARRI GÒTIC
C del Carme
Liceu
C de la Riera Alta
C de l'Hospital
Plaça del Pedró
EL RAVAL
C de la Cera
Rambla del Raval
Plaça de Salvador Seguí
C de Sant Pau
C Nou de la Rambla
La Rambla
Plaça de Josep Maria Folch i Torres
Plaça de Pere Coromines
Av de les Drassanes
Drassanes
Jardins de Sant Pau del Camp
Plaça del Portal de la Pau
Av del Paral·lel
Paral·lel
Jardins de les Tres Xemeneies
Plaça de les Drassanes
Port de Barcelona

Indoor & Outdoor GALLERIES

ART | CONTEMPORARY | URBAN

Art enthusiasts shouldn't miss a visit to Barcelona's Contemporary Art Museum, MACBA, or one of its contemporary art centres. However, in El Raval art is not just pieces locked in museums – it's everywhere. Stroll through this open-air street-art museum and you'll understand why the neighbourhood lives and breathes art.

ALLARD ONE/SHUTTERSTOCK ©

How to

Getting here The metro stations of Universitat, Liceu, Drassanes and Sant Antoni border the neighbourhood.

When to go Come during the day, preferably from Wednesday to Sunday to avoid some museum closures.

Tip Crowds of skaters gather all day, every day of the week in front of MACBA and offer a very interesting scene to watch, perhaps from one of the restaurant terraces at Kino or Doña Rosa.

ARCHITECT: JOSEP LLUÍS MATEO; XAVI TORRENT/GETTY IMAGES ©

Contemporary Art Spaces

Barcelona Contemporary Art Museum (MACBA) Spend an entire morning or afternoon visiting and understanding the extensive collection of contemporary art by international artists in a building that's a work of art on its own, and stands out against the older examples of architecture in the neighbourhood.

MACBA features a permanent collection of over 5000 works as well as temporary exhibitions. The art spans the second half of the 20th century up to the present day, although some works of the 1920s avant-garde movement are also present and serve as an introduction to the rest of the collection.

All exhibitions can be visited for free every Saturday after 4pm, and tours are often guided by the artists themselves.

GIMAS/SHUTTERSTOCK ©

A Space for Film Enthusiasts

Pop into **Filmoteca de Catalunya** for a film exhibition or screening among local film lovers. The aim of this space is to preserve and promote film culture, and it features different exhibition rooms, projection rooms, a library and a bookshop.

Top left Barcelona Contemporary Art Museum (MACBA), by architect Richard Meier **Above** Filmoteca de Catalunya **Left** *Luis Claramunt: The Vertical Journey* exhibition at MACBA

Centre for Contemporary Culture (CCCB) Come here for temporary exhibitions with a focus on the city, urban culture and public spaces, as well as an experimental film and contemporary culture archive. The aim of the centre is to encourage research, debate and dissemination of contemporary culture.

Different art forms come together at CCCB, from visual arts to transmedia, literature, music, film and philosophy. Festivals, workshops and events are also common at the centre, which is located in the building of an old almshouse, **Casa de Caritat**.

Virreina Palace This flamboyant building's name can be literally translated as 'vicereine's palace'. It was built between 1772 and 1778 by the viceroy of Peru and named after his wife. Today it hosts the **Centre de la Imatge** or 'image centre', which specialises in contemporary art and, more specifically, the use of images as a source of knowledge and cultural experiences.

Street Art Top 3

Jardins de les Tres Xemeneies Barcelona's ever-changing outdoor gallery is a must see. The free-for-all policy attracts artists of all styles and status from every part of the world.

Keith Haring's 'Todos Juntos Podemos Parar el SIDA' Don't miss the legendary artist's gift to Barcelona, whose powerful social message still rings true today. Located on a concrete wall near the entrance of MACBA.

MeLata Always look up! You will find amazing hidden art when you do. These recycled cans painted with upbeat words feature beautiful messages to inspire the people of Barcelona.

Recommended by Jimi Suárez. *Jimi is a former street-art tour guide at Artspace Tours. @jimi_suarez_1503*

Left *Todos Juntos Podemos Parar el SIDA* by Keith Haring **Below** Centre for Contemporary Culture (CCCB), by architects Helio Piñón and Albert Viaplana

Different spaces in the building are used for multiple art and photography exhibitions, as well as seminars, talks and workshops. A visit to this space will be of interest to anyone, but particularly for photography enthusiasts. Admission is always free.

Street Art in Barcelona

Barcelona has been a playground for street artists for years, and some of the best examples of street art in the city can be found in El Raval.

Carrer de l'Aurora On this street a space called **Àgora Juan Andrés Benítez** was created to honour a neighbour who died here in a controversial dispute with the police, the story of which is told through the graffiti on the walls.

Let a street artist show you around The best way to fully immerse yourself in street art is to join a street-art tour such as that offered by **BeLocal Tours**, where you get to walk around El Raval with a street artist who will explain some of the most notable works to be found around the area. After the tour, you'll get to practise your street-art skills during a graffiti workshop.

08 Lively MARKETS

FOOD | VINTAGE | SHOPPING

Make your way through the vibrant stalls of La Boqueria Market to understand and taste the flavours of the region, whether it's at some of the stalls or at one of the excellent tapas bars in the market. El Raval is also paradise for vintage and antique lovers, with many shops and even some markets selling items salvaged from another time.

SORBIS/SHUTTERSTOCK ©

How to

Getting here The nearest metro station is Liceu.

When to go The best time to visit food markets is in the morning, when all of the stalls are open.

Finger food If you get hungry you can find finger food and snacks in some of the stalls, or you can head to one of the tapas bars located inside the market.

Fun tip Different tour companies offer La Boqueria market tours and cooking workshops, a great way to taste the local ingredients and learn some recipes to cook back home.

ELENA ROSTUNOVA/SHUTTERSTOCK ©

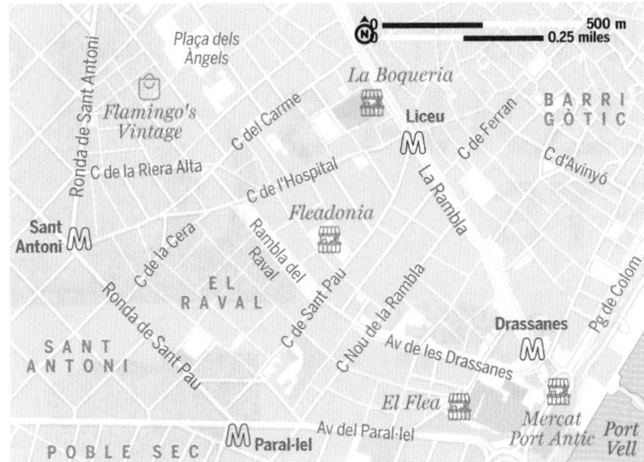

Not Just a Tourist Attraction

While it is true that the market has earned a reputation for being a tourist hotspot, attracting millions of visitors yearly, La Boqueria has always remained a true, quality, fresh-food market that's still frequented by many locals. Its produce is mostly sourced regionally, but some exotic products can also be found in the market's nearly 300 stalls.

Admire the Entrance & the Metal Frame

Before stepping in, take a moment to appreciate the big metal frame that houses the market, which was finished in 1914 and was typical of modernist architecture of the time. The entrance arch, which adds a small touch of colour to the structure, features an old coat of arms of the city.

Release Your Inner Foodie & Explore the Stalls

Many of the stalls of La Boqueria have existed for ages, and it is not uncommon for some of them to be passed on from one generation to the next. The most popular market stalls include fresh fruits and vegetables, meats, cheese, cold cuts, poultry and eggs, fish and seafood, olives and nuts.

Grab a Seat at these Bars for a Tapa & a Drink

El Quim de La Boqueria An icon of the market. Among the excellent tapas, the fried eggs with baby squid are a must-try.

Bar Pinotxo Famous for its chickpea dish, as well as many other meat and seafood options.

Kiosko Universal The place to go for fresh, quality seafood prepared right in front of you.

Left Butcher stall at La Boqueria
Bottom left Mercat Port Antic

Vintage & Antiques

Mercat Port Antic Also known as 'Mercat de Colom' because of its location right next to the Columbus Monument, this weekly flea market has collector's items of all sorts.

Fleadonia & El Flea 'One man's garbage is another man's gold' is the motto of this secondhand market where the main items are vintage clothes, accessories and vinyl. Markets normally take place on the first and the second Sunday of the month.

Flamingo's Vintage With three different locations selling American vintage fashion in great condition, this is an amusing place to shop secondhand. Items can be bought individually or by the kilogram, starting at €13 per kilo.

What you'll find in **BARCELONA'S MARKETS**

01 Ham and cold cuts

Different types of ham, from serrano ham to fine acorn-fed Iberian ham, cold cuts and sausages.

02 Fuet

A staple of Catalan gastronomy, *fuet* is a thin pork sausage that's seasoned and dry-cured.

03 Cheese

There's a whole world of cheese to discover beyond manchego, such as the local varieties *mató,* Alt Urgell and Garrotxa.

04 Nougat

This popular Spanish sweet made with nuts, egg whites and honey is eaten especially at Christmas. A popular local variety is *torró d'Agramunt.*

05 Meat

One thing you will always find at any food market is stalls selling a wide variety of meat types and cuts.

06 Fish and seafood

An important part of the local diet, the quality and variety of seafood found in local markets is extraordinary.

07 Candied fruit

The most colourful stalls are those selling these sweet fruit bites, which are drenched in syrup to preserve them.

08 Nuts

Walnuts, almonds, chestnuts, hazelnuts, pine nuts, peanuts, pistachios... Nut stalls sometimes also sell dried fruits, such as dates, as well as chocolates.

09 Wild mushrooms

Delicious, varied fresh mushrooms during autumn, as well as dried wild mushrooms and truffle products all year round.

10 Olives

Massive buckets containing kilos of different olive varieties, which can be found whole, pitted, stuffed and seasoned.

11 Preserved food

From peppers to anchovies, tuna, sardines, mussels and cockles, preserved using oil or vinegar.

12 Salted fish

Fish such as codfish and sardines are preserved using salt. Salted codfish is sold both in bigger pieces and in smaller strips.

09 Diverse Dining & DRINKING

MELTING POT | CULTURE | FOOD

From migrants to students, artists and young professionals, there's something about this corner of the city that attracts diversity and promotes coexistence. Food and drinks commonly bring people together, and that's definitely the case here. Explore El Raval through its diverse offering of restaurants and bars and get to meet the neighbours.

How to

Getting around El Raval is best explored on foot, so put your comfortable shoes on!

When to go It's best to avoid walking around the area late at night.

Tip If you're open to everything, the neighbourhood boasts an incredible number of exotic restaurants and food shops.

Rambla del Raval: the Neighbourhood's Heart

After stopping to appreciate the iconic monument named Botero's Cat, head to some of these venues that represent El Raval's diversity:

La Poderosa A colourful little take-away shop selling Venezuelan specialties.

Paloma Blanca Small, no-frills Moroccan restaurant serving seafood platters, couscous and other traditional dishes.

El Pachuco Mexican food and drinks in an atmosphere that feels like taking a quick trip to the other side of the world.

Top right Fonda España
Right Granja M. Viader

ALBUM/ALAMY STOCK PHOTO ©

MAZUR TRAVEL/SHUTTERSOCK ©

Ølgod Craft Beer Bar
Featuring 30 taps with international and local brews, an industrial design, food and great vibes.

Trendy Spots on Carrer de Joaquín Costa

Continue your journey by bar-hopping on Carrer de Joaquín Costa, where groups of 20- and 30-somethings come for the casually cool atmosphere.

Two Schmucks Opened by two friends who just wanted to serve great cocktails in a fun way. This place was recently voted one of the best cocktail bars in the world.

3345 Bar & Gallery A wide, industrial space serving food and drinks paired with occasional art displays.

Old-School Gems

Casa Almirall Founded in 1860 and decorated in art-nouveau style, it's the perfect place to enjoy a drink and travel back to other times.

Granja M. Viader Opened in 1870 as a milk shop, today it serves pastries, churros and sandwiches, as well as its famous chocolate milk.

Fonda España Traditional Catalan cuisine with a contemporary twist in a modernist dining room.

Unravelling El Raval

THE HISTORY BEHIND BARCELONA'S MOST DIVERSE NEIGHBOURHOOD

El Raval never really enjoyed a good reputation, at least until recent years. Issues such as degradation, crime and prostitution have affected the neighbourhood for hundreds of years, but the 21st century seems to be shaping a very different story for this long-neglected part of the city.

Left Sant Pau del Camp
Middle Hospital de la Santa Creu
Right Jardins de Rubió i Lluch

SKOVALSKY/SHUTTERSTOCK ©

An Outer Suburb

El Raval was not part of the original core of the city. Up until the 14th century it was just a rural area of farming land. The oldest building here is the **Sant Pau del Camp** monastery and church, a Romanesque construction estimated to date to the late 9th century.

Addition to the Medieval City

In the 14th century, new city walls were built in addition to the existing ones to include part of modern-day Raval. There were different reasons behind this, but the main one related to the plague that had affected the city during previous years. El Raval was designed to be an area where, apart from farming land that could feed the city in case of sieges and plagues, a hospital and a leprosarium could also be built where the sick population could stay apart from the rest of the city.

The area became, therefore, a place not only for unwanted people but also illicit pursuits such as prostitution and other illegal activities.

It was soon after this expansion that the **Hospital de la Santa Creu** (Hospital of the Holy Cross) was built. In use until 1929, it was the place where Gaudí spent his last days. From the 16th century onwards the area became a popular location for convents, such as **Convent dels Àngels** and **Convent de Santa Mònica**.

Between the 18th and 19th centuries, due to the low population density in the area, El Raval was chosen as the location for the construction of numerous factories in the city, especially in the textile industry. El Raval became a

STEFANO POLITI MARKOVINA/ALAMY STOCK PHOTO ©

MICK2770/SHUTTERSTOCK ©

neighbourhood of factories and factory workers, and it would also become the scene of upheavals and confrontations in succeeding years.

The 'Chinatown' of Barcelona

In the early 1900s, El Raval attracted great artists of the time, who were fascinated by the underground atmosphere of the neighbourhood and its cabarets, brothels and taverns. In 1925 the name 'Chinatown' was first used by a journalist to describe the neighbourhood by comparing it to New York's Chinatown, a name that would stick up until the 1980s.

El Raval in the 21st Century

After the civil war, a time when the neighbourhood's reputation had sunk even more, transformations finally started to take place, especially during the 1992 Olympics. By the turn of the 21st century, El Raval was experiencing a resurgence like never before. Today the neighbourhood is home to people who come from all corners of the world, with an estimated 61% of the population having been born abroad. This diversity applies not only to people's origins but can also be seen in its shops, restaurants, art scene, events, cultural offerings and more. There is no doubt that El Raval has seen a spectacular transformation throughout the years, which, judging by the area's vibrant energy, will continue to shape its future.

By the turn of the century, El Raval was experiencing a resurgence like never before.

A Peaceful Oasis in El Raval

The little oasis of peace and green that is **Jardins de Rubió i Lluch** is in the middle of the densely populated Raval, surrounded by the Gothic buildings that once housed the Hospital de la Santa Creu. A fountain at its centre provides the relaxing backdrop of running water, with orange trees completing the scene. It's common to spot small groups of neighbours playing chess here.

Located in the courtyard, **El Jardí** is a bar with a lively terrace serving coffee, drinks, tapas and other food. The bar doesn't offer particularly special dishes, but the atmosphere truly makes up for it.

Listings

BEST OF THE REST

 Traces of Medieval History

Jardins del Baluard

Literally translated as 'gardens of the bastion', this is located on one of the 11 bastions that were part of Barcelona's city wall.

Maritime Museum

Showcasing the history of shipping in Barcelona, this museum features some impressive replicas and explores the importance of this activity throughout the city's history.

Old Hospital de la Santa Creu

A fascinating Gothic building dating back to the 15th century and in use until 1929, the complex was created in order to merge six hospitals. Today it houses different cultural institutions.

Performance Centres & Art Galleries

BARTS

Acronym for Barcelona Arts on Stage, this venue has two event rooms that host an interesting range of performances, from concerts of all kinds to festivals, theatre, comedy and dance.

Miscelanea

An art gallery showcasing works from around the world, but especially local talents. It's also a space for workshops and events, with its own little cafe and a shop selling mainly prints.

Cooking Workshops & Experiences With Locals

Paella Club

Where paella fanatics can learn how to cook this traditional dish in a fun setting. Speakeasy cocktail class and tapas tasting, as well as brunch cooking, are also part of the workshop offerings.

Uncensored Barcelona Tour

Dive deep into El Raval's past and present and learn about the social and political happenings that have shaped the neighbourhood. Tours offer a very local, insider's perspective.

 Tapas, Veggie Hotspots, Modern & World Cuisine

Bar Cañete €€

Some of the best classic-style tapas in town, featuring a long bar where customers can watch the kitchen in action. Bar Cañete attracts a big crowd and is loved by locals.

La Paradeta Paral·lel €€

The place to eat fresh seafood in the area. This unpretentious restaurant has some of the freshest seafood, all displayed for you to choose and priced by weight at very budget-friendly prices.

Dos Pebrots €€€

Modern Catalan cuisine made to impress. Every dish is carefully considered, made and plated. You won't have dinner, you'll go on a culinary journey.

Frankie Gallo Cha Cha Cha €€

Superb pizzas in a wide space with vintage industrial decor, neon lights, music and a fun vibe. Craft beers and flavourful Italian desserts complete the menu.

Makan Makan €€

Southeast Asian food served in a small yet cosy space. The menu includes classics from countries such as Indonesia and Thailand.

Veggie Garden €

Vegan, tasty meals and dishes from around the world, served in generous portions. Great for a low-budget lunch or dinner, with a daily set menu available for under €10.

Bar Central Raval €€

This bar, located on a quiet street of El Raval, shares the space with a bookstore. A laid-back oasis of green where you can stop to rest before continuing to explore the area.

Speciality Coffee & Unique Bites

Chök The Chocolate Kitchen €

Chocolate lovers will enjoy visiting this chocolate workshop and store where they'll find gourmet doughnuts, chocolates, cupcakes and more, attractively displayed.

Dalston Coffee €

This small speciality coffee shop, with an entrance decorated with colourful graffiti art, is renowned for its great coffee, to go or to enjoy at one of the few tables outside.

Old-School, Panoramic & Music Bars

La Confiteria €€

A modernist cocktail bar with beautiful tiled floors, a long wooden bar and attractive cocktail presentations. The vintage feels are everywhere, starting with the old-school facade.

Bar Marsella €

Open since 1820, the slightly run-down decor here adds to the bohemian ambience. It is said to have been frequented by the likes of Picasso and Hemingway and is famous for its absinthe.

Big Bang Bar €

Popular for its live music and open-mic nights, at this friendly bar you can usually catch live jam sessions – and take part in one, if you're up for it – from Wednesday to Sunday.

JONATHAN STOKES/LONELY PLANET ©

Bar Marsella

360º Terrace €€

A fancy option for those who would like to enjoy a cocktail with breathtaking 360-degree views of the city at a hotel rooftop bar.

Vintage & Unique Shops

Carrer dels Tallers

A side street off La Rambla, this is a popular street for those looking for vintage items, including vinyl shops and preloved fashion stores.

Revólver Records

This shop, beloved by collectors and vinyl enthusiasts, sells an immense variety of independent records, both secondhand and new.

Fantastik

Entering this store is like stepping into a colourful and kitsch fantasy world. Fantastik sells unique gifts and funky items from around the world.

Holala!

With two locations a minute away from each other, the selection of unique vintage clothes sold by Holala! is really appreciated by retro-clothing fanatics.

Scan to find more things to do in El Raval online

MARIA SHIPAKINA/SHUTTERSTOCK ©

LA RIBERA
Trip Builder

TAKE YOUR PICK OF MUST-SEES AND HIDDEN GEMS

La Ribera is a former merchants' district, today home to concept stores and art galleries hidden among the narrow alleys that form the medieval quarter. Packed with buildings from the 14th century, this historical district also houses the Picasso Museum, the modernist Palau de la Música Catalana and Parc de la Ciutadella, the lungs of downtown.

Neighbourhood Notes

Best for Medieval architecture, parks, museums, music, vintage shopping.

Transport Jaume I or Barceloneta metro stations.

Getting around Explore on foot.

Note El Born is part of La Ribera and the full name of the neighbourhood is La Ribera, Santa Caterina i Sant Pere, which acknowledges its three sections.

Listen to a classical-music concert in a remarkable modernist building at **Palau de la Música Catalana**.
8 mins from Jaume I metro station

Urquinaona

Via Laietana

Get a hint of Picasso's earlier years and his life in Barcelona at **Museu Picasso**.
4 mins from Jaume I metro station

BARRI GÒTIC

Get fashionable by shopping at one of the many vintage stores such as **Le Swing Vintage**.
3 mins from Jaume I metro station

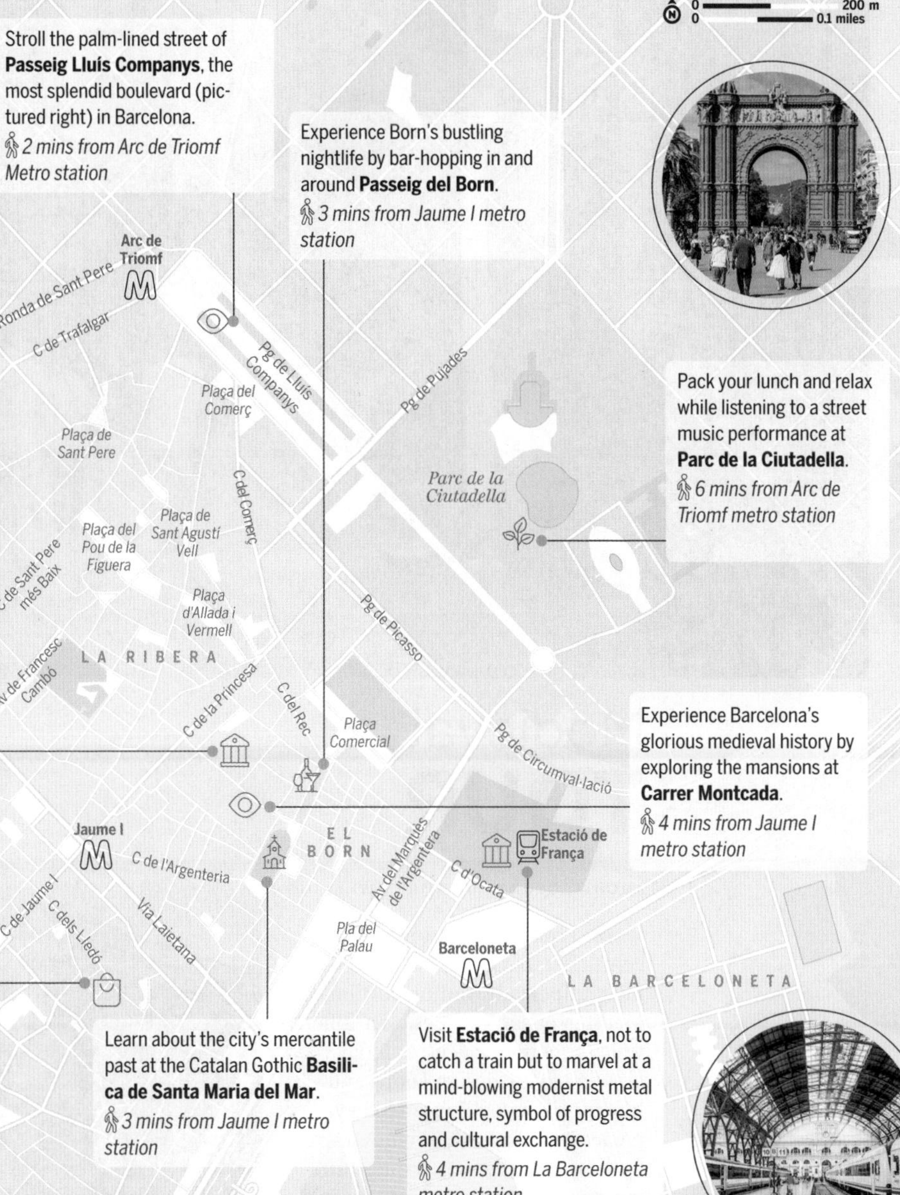

Stroll the palm-lined street of **Passeig Lluís Companys**, the most splendid boulevard (pictured right) in Barcelona.
2 mins from Arc de Triomf Metro station

Experience Born's bustling nightlife by bar-hopping in and around **Passeig del Born**.
3 mins from Jaume I metro station

Pack your lunch and relax while listening to a street music performance at **Parc de la Ciutadella**.
6 mins from Arc de Triomf metro station

Experience Barcelona's glorious medieval history by exploring the mansions at **Carrer Montcada**.
4 mins from Jaume I metro station

Learn about the city's mercantile past at the Catalan Gothic **Basilica de Santa Maria del Mar**.
3 mins from Jaume I metro station

Visit **Estació de França**, not to catch a train but to marvel at a mind-blowing modernist metal structure, symbol of progress and cultural exchange.
4 mins from La Barceloneta metro station

10 Medieval TOUR

ARCHITECTURE | HISTORY | WALKING

From the 13th to the 15th centuries, Barcelona became the most important trading port on the Mediterranean coast and La Ribera was its economic centre. Today, among trendy design shops and hipster bars, you'll find medieval palaces, mansions and churches built by wealthy merchants and guilds to confront and undermine the abuses of the noble class.

ALEXEY PEVNEV/SHUTTERSTOCK ©

How to

Getting there and around Jaume I or Barceloneta metro stations. The area is best explored on foot.

When to go Avoid crowds by going early in the morning.

Mercat de Santa Caterina While not part of the medieval tour, the local market is a great place to stop for breakfast, lunch, or even a *canya*. For a local-like atmosphere, go to Bar Joan, inside the market.

ALEXEY PEVNEV/SHUTTERSTOCK ©

JOAN_BAUTISTA/SHUTTERSTOCK ©

The origin of the merchants' industry
Rec Comtal was an irrigation channel built in the 10th century to supply the city with water, around which water mills were built. Some of them were constructed in today's **Plaça Sant Agustí Vell**, and these were the mills artisan weavers used to produce their cloth. That was just the beginning of an industry that later evolved into the most prominent on the Mediterranean Sea. You may notice that Plaça Sant Agustí Vell has a slight inclination – that's because it was built on ground that followed the water course. Those interested in this history can have a look at a slice of Rec Comtal in the **El Born Centre de Cultura i Memòria** (Born CCM).

The guilds that made La Ribera
With some proficiency in Catalan, you may realise that many streets in La Ribera have

The First Public Bank in the World

In response to the unprecedented crisis caused by the Black Death, Barcelona created Taula de Canvis, the first public bank in the world. Located inside La Llotja, its mission was to fund large trading projects overseas, at a time where there wasn't any money to fund them.

Top left Carrer de Montcada
Left La Llotja de Mar de Barcelona
Above John the Baptist statue at Carrer Assaonador 1

trade names: Sombrerers, Espaseria, Vidrieria or Mercaders. In the medieval era these streets were grouped by guilds, and still carry their names today. Keen observers may be able to find actual references from that era. For example, **Carrer Assaonador 1** (Tanners) still preserves a statue of John the Baptist, the patron saint of that particular guild; or **Carrer Carders 45-46-47** (Wool Carders) features a plaque stating that the current 18th-century building was built over the former guild hall.

Carrer Montcada Dating back to the 12th century, Carrer Montcada was the lordliest of lordly streets in Barcelona, where the richest merchants built their presumptuous residences. Gothic and Renaissance palaces with stately staircases and courtyards all testify to the glorious past of medieval Barcelona. **Palau Aguilar**, **Palau Meca** and **Palau Baró de Castellet** are the finest examples, all of them housing the Picasso Museum.

Fossar de les Moreres

Adjacent to the Basilica de Santa Maria del Mar, there is a square named Fossar de les Moreres, literally Grave of the Mulberries, a memorial built over the cemetery of those who fell during the Barcelona siege (1713–14) in the War of the Spanish Succession, when Catalonia lost its institutions and autonomy. Today, this place has become the most important symbol for Catalan nationalism, but visitors should know that this site had been a cemetery since medieval times, way before the War of Succession and its subsequent patriotic association.

Recommended by Maria López
Maria is a Barcelona guide.
@basilicasantamariadelmar

Left Fossar de les Moreres
Below Palau Episcopal de Barcelona, Carrer del Bisbe

La Llotja de Mar de Barcelona The barely visited and least known Gothic treasure in Barcelona is La Llotja de Mar, which was the institution, created in 1357, that served as a House of Trade for merchants. Nowadays, the exterior is Neoclassical but the interior has remained untouched, a luxurious three-nave Gothic salon whose arches still conserve the emblem of the Kingdom of Aragón. It is interesting to note that, up to 1970, it housed Escuela de Bellas Artes, a fine arts school that Pablo Picasso and Joan Miró attended. Previously arranged visits are possible (€12.90, llotjademar.cat/en/guided-tours).

Santa Maria del Mar The most important building is the Gothic Basílica de Santa Maria del Mar, built by the guilds and people of La Ribera. Entrance is free, but a separate ticket is required to visit the stands and crypt (€5) and rooftop (€10), from where you get a fantastic panoramic view of Barcelona. Guided visits are also available (one hour, €14, santamariadelmarbarcelona.org).

Basílica de Santa Maria del Mar

BY THE PEOPLE, FOR THE PEOPLE

Declared a basilica by the pope in 1923, Santa Maria del Mar is the most iconic medieval building in Barcelona, the emblem of Catalan Gothic, with its exceptional three naves merging in a wondrous simplicity, harmony and symmetry. It was also a direct witness to one of the most notable periods in the history of Barcelona.

Left *Bastaixos* figurines **Middle** The basilica's exterior **Right** Inside the basilica

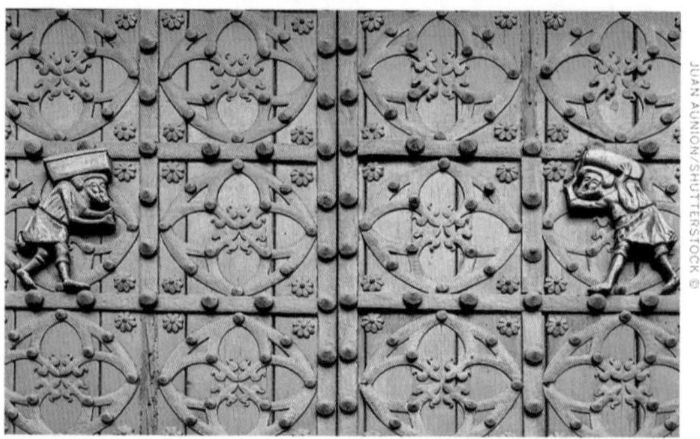

JUAN AUNION/SHUTTERSTOCK ©

The two small figurines embedded into the main entrance to the basilica illustrate the *bastaixos*, the porters who carried the heavy stones on their backs that would eventually give shape to the Gothic church. These *bastaixos* undertook the hardest work, the figurines being a recognition of that, but what makes Santa Maria del Mar particularly romantic is that its construction was also conducted by the sweat and tears of all the residents and merchants of La Ribera.

Rising Power of the Merchant Class

Barcelona at the beginning of the 14th century was part of the Kingdom of Aragon, and the city was going through the most prosperous time in its history, when entrepreneurs and visionaries from that era – sword makers, leather sellers and glass manufacturers – were benefiting enormously from a prosperous maritime trade. Wealth was increasing exponentially in La Ribera, where rich merchants spent their profits in adorning the district with luxurious mansions and Gothic buildings, making it the economic centre of the city of Barcelona.

Meanwhile, the Romanesque church of Santa Maria de les Arenes had been the main local Christian sanctuary for more than 300 years. While today's Gothic district held Barcelona's political and religious power, La Ribera was epicentre of financial power. The different guilds felt the old church didn't properly represent their power, and they perceived the politically funded Catedral de Barcelona as an alien temple.

DOMINGO LEIVA/GETTY IMAGES ©

PAOLO GALLO/SHUTTERSTOCK ©

Rivalling the Cathedral

In a spirit of competition with the adjacent locality, the guilds decided to build an ambitious Gothic church that would replace de les Arenes. The project was exclusively funded by the richest local families, built by the people, and designed by architects Berenguer de Montagut and Ramón Despuig.

From earthquakes to various wars and fires, the basilica has been the victim of numerous calamities.

The last stone was placed in 1383, just 53 years after construction began, an unprecedented timeframe for a work of this kind. The end result is an astonishing three-nave church characterised by the fact that its three naves are not cross-shaped and have similar heights, both elements from the Catalan Gothic.

FC Barcelona, Més Que un Club

From earthquakes to various wars and fires, the basilica has been the victim of numerous calamities throughout its seven centuries of history. These unfortunate events have required several restorations, the last of which took place in the 1960s, when the stained-glass windows damaged during the civil war were restored. Eagle-eyed visitors may notice that on the left side of the basilica, looking down onto the altar, one of the 2nd-floor windows features the Barça emblem, deliberately placed there as FC Barcelona funded part of that restoration.

Basílica Myths

The popular novel's title *Catedral del Mar* gives the wrong idea that the church is a cathedral, but it's actually a basilica. Also the novel tries to romanticise the idea that *bastaixos* brought the stones by foot from Montjuïc, but they were actually taken by boat, at a time where the seashore was much closer than it is now.

And it wasn't always as austere as it is today. During the last restoration, a significant part of the ornamentation was removed to make the basilica look even more austere, reinforcing the idea that Catalan Gothic was more unique than it actually was.

By Sara Yelo,
Sara is a Barcelona guide. @basilica santamariadelmar

11 Concert at PALAU

ARCHITECTURE | HISTORY | MUSIC

Dreamed up by the architect Lluís Domènech i Montaner in 1905, Palau de la Música Catalana is an exceptional outburst of modernist architecture, a progressive and UNESCO-listed concert hall decorated with awe-inspiring natural forms and ornaments, offering not only the chance to hear some of the world's top artists, but also a mystical experience.

How to

Getting there Urquinaona metro station.

When to go The official concert season runs from September to June. In summer, minor concerts are organised (especially flamenco), mainly targeting foreigners.

Tickets and prices Tickets can be bought on the official website (palaumusica.cat/en). Prices typically range from €12 to €150.

Visits Visiting the modernist building and its concert hall is also possible. A self-guided tour costs €10, guided visits €18.

A peculiar location The idea of building Palau de la Música was so it could serve as the headquarters for Orfeó Català, a choral society created in 1891 that, throughout the 20th century, became the cultural reference point for Catalan music and a symbol of Catalan nationalism. Visitors often wonder why the location chosen for such a building was one of the cramped streets of the medieval quarter instead of wide L'Eixample, but La Ribera was where Orfeó Català used to practise, plus they thought that the buildings across the street would be torn down in the near future, but they weren't. Some people claim it was a big mistake, while others

Top right Palau de la Música Catalana **Right** Hospital de Sant Pau

Hospital de Sant Pau

Palau de la Música is undoubtedly Muntaner's most remarkable work, but few know about Hospital de Sant Pau (santpaubarcelona.org/en/visits). Located in the district of Horta-Guinardó, this UNESCO World Heritage site and former hospital is composed of several modernist pavilions, making it the largest Catalan modernist work in the world. General admission is €10.50.

believe that its surroundings are what makes Palau de la Música unique and special.

Artists and music From classical composers like Enric Granados and Pau Casals to operatic sopranos like Montserrat Caballé and flamenco guitarists like Paco de Lucía, Palau de la Música has seen performances from the best Spanish artists of the 20th century, but it was never short of international artists either: Duke Ellington, Ella Fitzgerald, the London Philharmonic Orchestra and Michael Nyman are just a few examples of the diverse artists who have shown their skills within the walls of the Palau. Today, Palau de la Música is mostly known for its unbeatable classical music concerts, but, with over 300 concerts a year performed, they touch all genres, including flamenco, jazz and opera.

SOPOTNICKI/SHUTTERSTOCK ©

GAGLIARDIPHOTOGRAPHY/SHUTTERSTOCK ©

12 Picasso MUSEUM

HISTORY | ART | MUSEUM

Picasso was born in Málaga, but Barcelona was the city where he revealed himself as an artist, where he spent his adolescence, his youth, and his most crucial formative years. Spread across five medieval mansions from the 14th century, Museu Picasso displays the largest collection of his early works, while showcasing the emotional connection the artist had with the Mediterranean city.

MARCO RUBINO/SHUTTERSTOCK ©

How to

Getting there Jaume I is the closest metro station.

Tickets General admission costs €12, which includes the permanent collection and temporary exhibition. To avoid unnecessary queues, book tickets online at museupicasso.bcn.cat/en

Get in for free Entrance is free on Thursday, from 5pm to 8pm; the first Sunday of every month; and on 12 Februar, 18 May and 24 September. Capacity is limited, so booking a few days in advance is recommended.

PIT STOCK/SHUTTERSTOCK ©

Pablo Picasso and Barcelona Picasso moved to Barcelona in 1895, at the age of 14, and he lived here permanently until 1904, when he moved to Paris. Those years formed him not only as an artist but also as an individual, which explains why Picasso never stopped coming back to visit his friends and circle of artists. He always acknowledged the affection he had for Barcelona, visible in the hundreds of works he donated and, most importantly, in the creation of Museu Picasso, which he founded in 1963, with the help of his close friend and secretary Jaume Sabartés.

Els Quatre Gats Literally 'Four Cats', this modernist building used to be a bar and cabaret known for its bohemian and progressive atmosphere, frequented by the most important artists, including Picasso. The bar shut its doors in 1903 to become the headquarters of an art society, but the civil war and subsequent dictatorship put an end to that. It remained closed until 1989, when a local family restored it to open a chic cafe and restaurant that serves traditional Catalan food, but they have kept the feel and atmosphere that used to prevail here. It's at Carrer Montsió 3, 10 minutes on foot from Museu Picasso.

Curious fact Picasso's views opposing Franco's dictatorial regime were widely known and that's why, in fear of it being censored, the museum was named Col·lecció Sabartés.

Left & bottom left The museum's inner courtyard

Picasso Collection Highlights

Don't expect to see the best Picassos here, but rather the incredible talent he had at a young age. The museum displays more than 4000 works, the vast majority pre-1904, but there are also works from his later periods.

Earliest works (1890–1901) Characterised by his representations of landscapes, portraits and scenes from everyday life. *Aunt Pepa* (1896) and *Science and Charity* (1897) are fine examples.

Blue Period (1901–04) Paintings dominated by blue tonalities, transmitting decadence and sadness. Don't miss *Woman with a Bonnet* (1901) and *Barcelona Rooftops* (1903).

Meninas de Velázquez (1957) View 58 cubist interpretations of Velázquez's famous painting, *Las Meninas*.

13 Food TOUR

FOOD | LOCAL LIFE | RESTAURANTS

La Ribera is one of Barcelona's most touristy districts, so finding a decent restaurant that's popular with locals can be a challenge. But if you know where to go, you can eat your way around El Born with culinary delights for every meal of the day.

FERRAN LOZANO CUSI/SHUTTERSTOCK ©

Trip Notes

Getting here Metro to Jaume I and Barceloneta.

Getting around El Born is best explored on foot.

Esmorzar de forquilla Catalans are not big morning eaters, but some 'truly local' places specialise in hearty breakfasts, locally named as *esmorzar de forquilla* (fork breakfast) and typically consisting of *cap i pota* (pictured above; veal head and leg), *fricandó* (beef stew) or *bacallà* (cod fish).

Menú del día A €10–15 lunch deal offered by most local restaurants, mainly on weekdays.

Spanish Meal Times

There are five official meals in Spain, but Spaniards don't necessarily have them all in one day. *Desayuno* (light breakfast) at 8am; *almuerzo* (late, hearty breakfast) at 10.30am; *vermut* (pre-lunch, light meal) at 1pm; *comida* (lunch) at 2.30pm; *merienda* or *aperitivo de la tarde* (afternoon snack) at 7pm; *cena* (dinner) at 10pm.

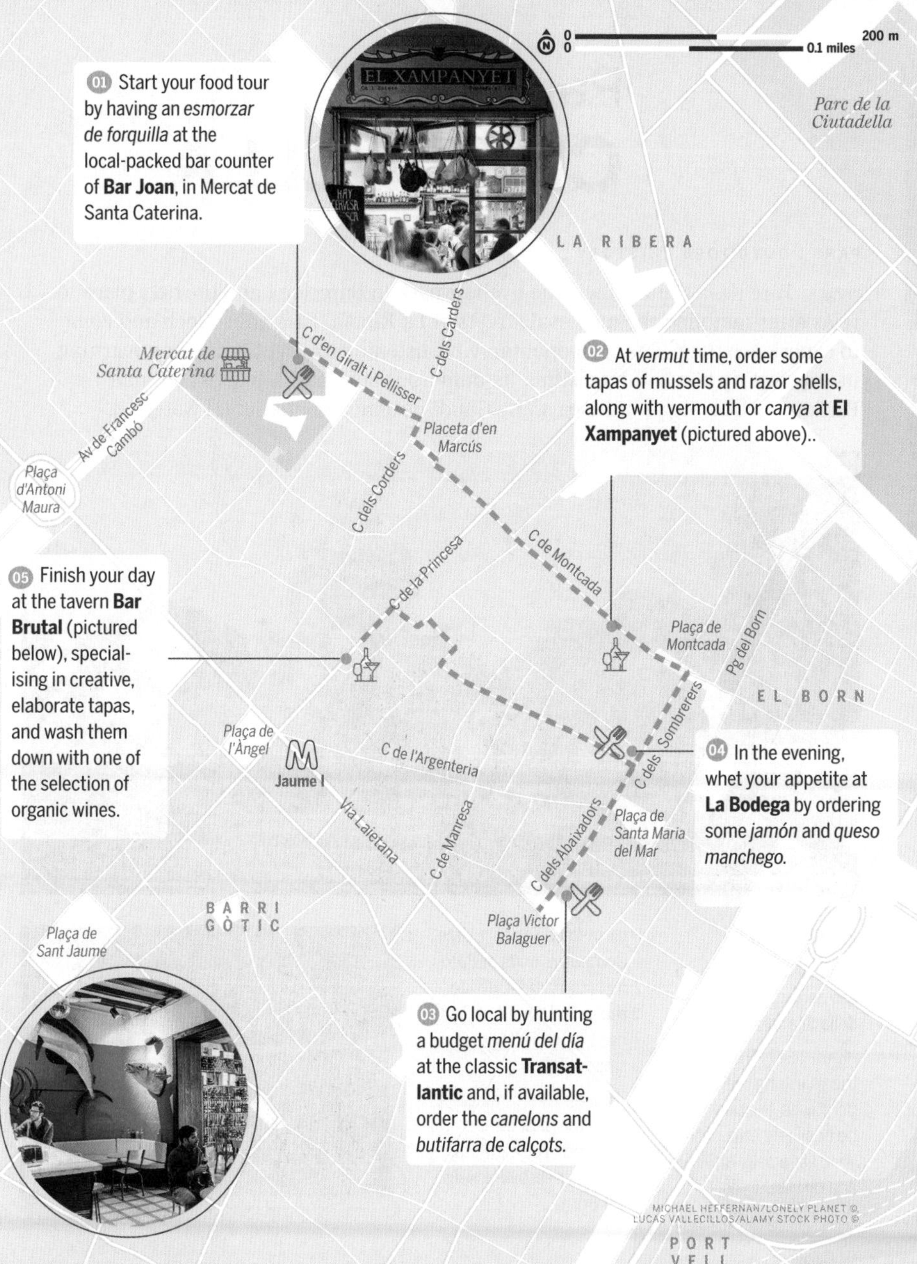
0
0
200 m
0.1 miles
01 Start your food tour by having an *esmorzar de forquilla* at the local-packed bar counter of **Bar Joan**, in Mercat de Santa Caterina.
EL XAMPANYET
HAY CERVESA
Parc de la Ciutadella
LA RIBERA
C dels Carders
C d'en Giralt i Pellisser
Mercat de Santa Caterina
02 At *vermut* time, order some tapas of mussels and razor shells, along with vermouth or *canya* at **El Xampanyet** (pictured above)..
Av de Francesc Cambó
Placeta d'en Marcús
Plaça d'Antoni Maura
C dels Corders
C de Montcada
C de la Princesa
05 Finish your day at the tavern **Bar Brutal** (pictured below), specialising in creative, elaborate tapas, and wash them down with one of the selection of organic wines.
Plaça de Montcada
Pg del Born
EL BORN
C dels Sombrerers
Plaça de l'Àngel
Jaume I
C de l'Argenteria
04 In the evening, whet your appetite at **La Bodega** by ordering some *jamón* and *queso manchego*.
Via Laietana
C de Manresa
C dels Abaixadors
Plaça de Santa Maria del Mar
BARRI GÒTIC
Plaça Victor Balaguer
Plaça de Sant Jaume
03 Go local by hunting a budget *menú del día* at the classic **Transatlantic** and, if available, order the *canelons* and *butifarra de calçots*.
PORT VELL

14 Parc de la CIUTADELLA

PARK | OUTDOORS | HISTORY

Parc de la Ciutadella is the liveliest park in Barcelona and the best place to relax after rambling the medieval streets of La Ribera. Pack your lunch and come to experience the park's cosmopolitan vibe, listening to street musicians, learning its captivating history and visiting its numerous landmarks, like the Catalan Parliament, the zoo and the partially Gaudí-designed monumental waterfall.

BRIDGETOHORIZON/SHUTTERSTOCK ©

How to

Getting there Metro to Arc de Triomf and Ciutadella Vila Olímpica.

When to go Thanks to the year-long mild temperatures, the park can be busy any time of the year, especially after 6pm and on weekends.

Hidden gems Strollable, palm-lined Passeig Lluís Companys ends at Parc de la Ciutadella. Inside the park, Barcelona Zoo has been thrilling visitors since 1892.

Closing times You can't be in the park after 10.30pm. For nightlife, head to nearby Passeig del Born.

JOAN_BAUTISTA/SHUTTERSTOCK ©

A symbol of Catalan identity The National Day of Catalonia (11 September) memorialises the fall of the region during the War of the Spanish Succession in 1714, when Catalans lost their institutions. Shortly after his victory in 1715, Philip V of Spain ordered the building of a citadel around the city to keep *barcelonins* under his control. That citadel became a symbol of repression until it was demolished during the Spanish Revolution of 1868. The waste ground resulting from that demolition is where the Parc de la Ciutadella was built, hence its name, literally 'Citadel's Park'.

The beginning of the fight for trans human rights In 1991, a group of neo-Nazis murdered Sonia Rescalvo Zafra in Parc de la Ciutadella, beating her to death merely for her gender identity. Such an unfortunate event caused a lot of controversy in a country where there wasn't much awareness about transgender rights yet. The murder became the turning point for reversing that. The music plaza where she was killed was named after her in 2013.

Cascada Monumental The most iconic element of the park is the monumental fountain, designed by the architect Josep Fontseré, though the hydraulic system was made by Antoni Gaudí. The monument is notable for its many sculptural ornaments.

Left The park's Cascada Monumental
Bottom left Barcelona Zoo

The Spain–Catalonia Conflict

One of the buildings in Parc de la Ciutadella that remains from the Philip V era is his arsenal, today the Parliament of Catalonia and the epicentre of the never-ending crisis between Catalonia and Spain. Locally known as *procés*, the conflict reached its climax in 2017, when Catalan leaders declared independence from the rest of Spain. Those actions led many of their leaders to jail, while others, like the former Catalan president, fled to Belgium or Switzerland, where they still reside. In 2021, the new progressive Spanish government granted presidential pardons to the imprisoned leaders, a first step in resolving a conflict that has been going for 10 years.

Listings

BEST OF THE REST

Budget International Eats

Costa Pacífico €

Authentic Mexican eatery specialising in ceviches and fish tacos. Its fried pescadillas are the best in town. Reservations are possible, but only indoors.

Red Ant €

The owners of always-crowded Mosquito opened this lesser-known, cosy, East Asian restaurant serving high-quality noodles and curries. Broad selection of craft beers. The home-made *mochis* are heavenly.

Koku Kitchen Buns €

This modern Japanese eatery is popular for its buns, aka Asian sandwiches, but the menu features *gyoza* and ramen as well.

NAP €

The name stands for Neapolitan Authentic Pizza and it claims to bake one of the best pizzas in Barcelona. Proof of that is that it's always packed with Italians.

Tlaxcal Cantina €

A gourmet, authentic *taquería* where you can taste plenty of non-Tex-Mex food, like *tacos de lengua* (tongue tacos) and *cochinita pibil* (marinated pork).

Tempting Tapas

El Xampanyet €

This traditional bar has been open since 1930. It does get busy, but the experience and food make the long wait absolutely worth it. Go local and order *mongetes de Santa Pau amb calamarcets* (Catalan beans with little squids) or *tripa de bacallà amb cigrons* (cod tripe with chickpeas).

Bar del Pla €

One of the few tapa bars in La Ribera still frequented by locals, and a Spanish bar where you can try all the classic tapas like *croquetas*, *ensaladilla* and *anchoas*.

Bar Joan €

Located inside Mercat de Santa Caterina and always packed with *barcelonins*, here you can try traditional food cooked with the freshest ingredients from the market. Best place for a hearty breakfast or a budget *menú del día*.

Bar Brutal/Can Cisa €€

A modern bodega with an extensive menu of organic wines, and abundant choices of creative fish tapas like smoked eel or razor clams with *calçots* (spring onions) and *romesco* (tomato-based sauce). The menu changes every season.

Bormuth €

This Spanish tapas bar has been here for ages and despite being always flooded with tourists, the quality hasn't decreased, and it still attracts a considerable number of locals. Well-served *canyes* (draught beer) and reasonably good *bravas* (potatoes in a spicy tomato sauce).

Cal Pep

La Bodega del Born €

There aren't many places left in El Born as authentic as La Bodega. It's the perfect place for some pre-lunch drinks, or an early, light dinner. It specialises in *embutidos* (Spanish cured meats) such as *jamón*, chorizo and *longaniza*, always with their respective portion of *pa amb tomàquet* (bread rubbed with tomato, olive oil and garlic).

Catalan Fine Dining

Fismuler €€€

Oysters and sea urchins, but also turbot with truffle or grilled fish with kimchi, are just some of the delicacies you can find in this creative Catalan restaurant.

Estimar €€€

Here you can try fresh fish coming directly from the port of Roses (Girona). Traditional grilled fish with a modern twist, cooked by chefs who worked in Michelin-star restaurants.

Cal Pep €€€

Another legendary restaurant in El Born that, despite the affluence of foreigners, still offers unrivalled quality. It specialises in seafood tapas, the classic ones, but with the freshest possible fish. The tortillas are also famous among *barcelonins.*

Hidden Bars

Cal Brut €

A local dive bar, very homey and well-priced for the area. It's attractively claustrophobic and decorated with Banksy graphics and photos of *Big Lebowski* characters. The food is OK, but you come here for the well-served *canyes* and friendly atmosphere.

Bar Mudanzas €

This used to be the classic, traditional Spanish bar for after-work *canyes* but, after closing permanently, it became a contemporary cocktail bar that kept the traditional decoration and essence from its previous life.

El Nus €

Some of the best-served *canyes* in La Ribera are offered in this old-school bar, hidden in one of the most cramped streets in the area. It has Czech beer on tap.

El Bar de l'Antic Teatre €

A terrace oasis hidden somewhere in the Old City, opened by a group of artists as a space for performing arts. Always packed with young 20-somethings.

Vintage Clothing & Accessories

Le Swing Vintage

This high-end vintage clothing shop is one of the pioneers in the sector, selling exclusive and singular pieces of clothing ranging from €29 to €1000.

KR Store

A temple for vintage clothing, opened by fashion designer Krizia Robustella. Shirts, leggings, overalls, jackets, caps, and everything in between, with extravagant but attractive designs.

Humana Vintage

Humana is a secondhand chain clothing store that opened a vintage branch at the heart of La Ribera. Come here for the cheapest vintage-style clothes.

La Clinique

'First-hand vintage rarities' is how this optical shop refers to the sunglasses its sells, also with perfumes and accessories.

Scan to find more things to do in La Ribera online

BARCELONETA & THE WATERFRONT

GASTRONOMY | HISTORY | OUTDOORS

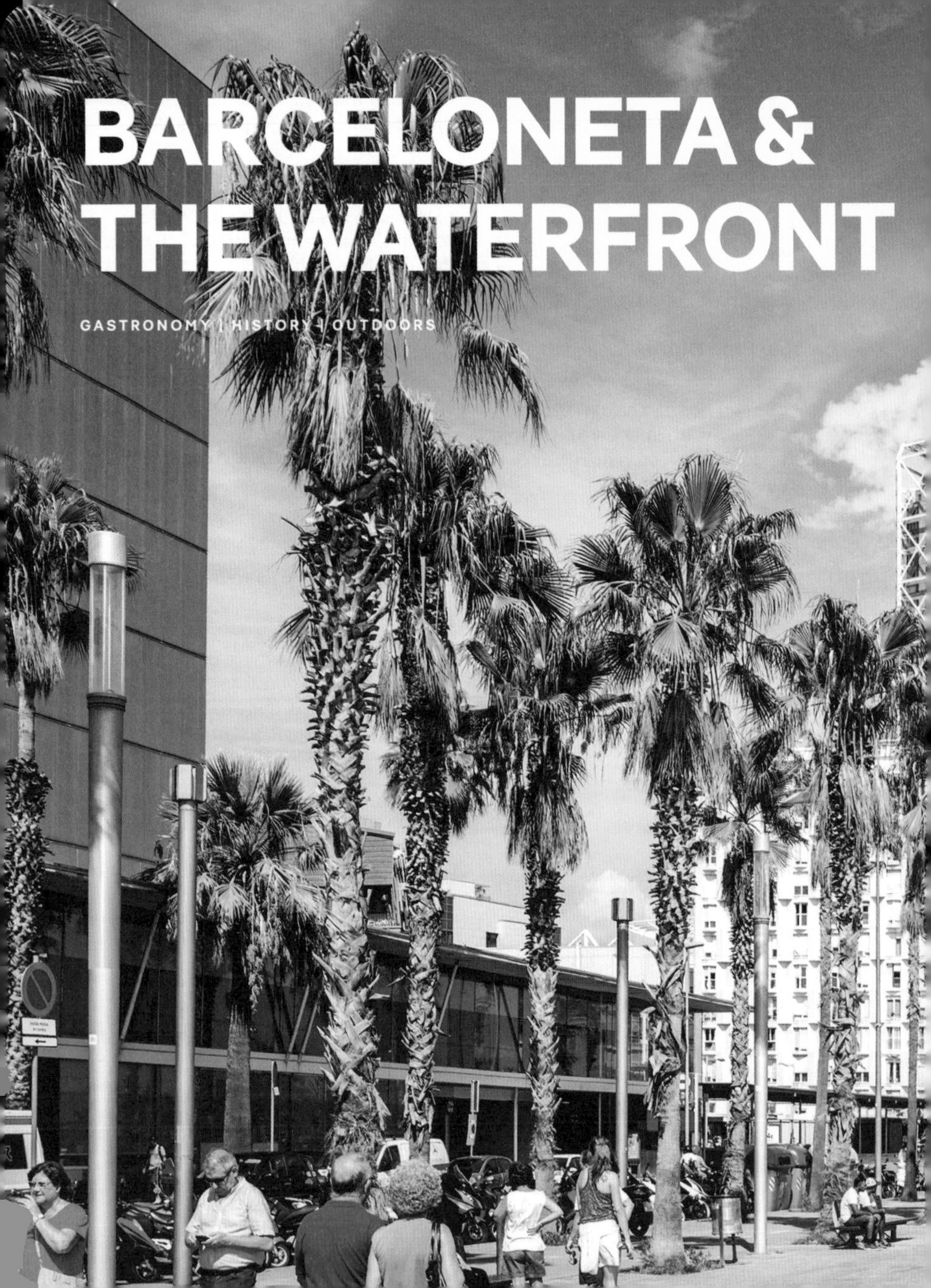

MAPFRE

BARCELONETA & THE WATERFRONT

Trip Builder

TAKE YOUR PICK OF MUST-SEES AND HIDDEN GEMS

Feeling lazy? Sporty? Hungry? Thirsty? Arty? Savvy? Barceloneta, the Waterfront and Poblenou areas can cover all your moods and needs, from taking a siesta on the beach, keeping fit on the promenade and tapas-hopping, to marvelling at art and history.

Neighbourhood Notes

Best for Vibrant beach life, hearty and hip bars and restaurants, heritage strolls.

Transport Barceloneta, Bogatell, Llacuna and Poblenou metro stations.

Getting around On foot with the Med breeze blowing on your face.

Tip Barceloneta is very popular among locals and tourists. Therefore, pickpocketing can happen. Be aware of your belongings at all times, especially when chilling on the beach or swimming in the sea.

Get your beach-picnic nibbles in **Mercat de la Barceloneta** and Baluard bakery.

5 mins from Barceloneta metro station

Dodge fixed-gear bikes and shopping trolleys in **Rambla de Poblenou**.

3 min from Poblenou metro station

Unleash your inner fitness freak on the waterfront – jog, cycle, surf, paddleboard, skate or work out at the **Nike Training Outdoor** area.

10 mins from Barceloneta metro station

Devour Barceloneta's ubiquitous bomba in **La Cova Fumada** bar.

8 mins from Barceloneta metro station

Sip on a sundowner at **La Guingueta de la Barceloneta** beach *xiringuito* bar.

10 mins from Barceloneta metro station

Use Rebecca Horn's **L'estel ferit sculpture** as your beach meeting point.

12 mins from Barceloneta metro station

15 The Great **OUTDOORS**

SPORT | FUN | BEACH LIFE

If you want to counteract the effects of gulping tapas and washing down vino, you're in the right place. Barceloneta and the Waterfront offer you plenty of options for fresh air and exercise on the Med.

PAGE LIGHT STUDIOS/SHUTTERSTOCK ©

How to

Getting here & around Barceloneta metro station is just a short distance from the Waterfront, where most bicycle and surfboard hire operators are located. Head to Poblenou metro station if your plans involve a kayak or a catamaran.

When to go There's activity all year round, but (surprise, surprise!) the Waterfront gets rammed in summer.

Get your gear on the spot Boardriders (Plaça del Mar 1-4) sells the sportswear that you forgot to pack at home.

Fit for the Waterfront

On land Happy on wheels? Improvise a cycling tour taking in boardwalks, sculptures, architecture and beaches along Barcelona's dynamic waterfront. Cycle on the dedicated **bike path** separated from traffic. It's flat and safe, but keep an eye out for pedestrians. Rather four wheels than two? There are two public **skate parks** along the waterfront: Mar Bella and Forum.

Up for a ball game? In Plaça del Poeta Boscà, Parc de la Barceloneta, Parc Carles I and Bogatell beach you'll find **ping pong tables**. If you prefer being closer to the sea, check if there's an available public **beach volleyball** sand court on Mar Bella, Nova Icària, Somorrostro or Barceloneta beaches. Hire a volleyball in Somorrostro's **Centre de la Platja** or just invite yourself to join a game with your friendliest smile.

More of a solo athlete? Start off at Rebecca Horn's *L'estel ferit* sculpture, which has become famous over the years as one of the most popular social meeting points in the city.

PAGE LIGHT STUDIOS/SHUTTERSTOCK ©

From here jog along the waterfront until you see the **Nike Training Outdoor** area, on the Espigó del Gas breakwater; it's a free-access calisthenics gym. You'll share the equipment with shirtless six-packs and beer bellies of all ages.

In the water The **Club Natació Atlètic-Barceloneta** (Plaça del Mar) has one indoor and two outdoor pools, spa, gym, paddle-tennis courts, solarium and private beach access. Day passes are available for €13.45. In **Base Nàutica Municipal** (Avinguda del Litoral) you can take kayaking, windsurfing and catamaran sailing lessons as well as hire equipment. SUP and surfing are your thing? Head to **Molokai Center** (Carrer de Meer 39), **Manihi Surf School** (Carrer de Meer 49) or **Surf House Barcelona** (Carrer Emília Llorca Martín 22). SUP and yoga at the same time? Sure, no problem. In **Club Patí Vela**

Made-in-Barceloneta Beach Sport

Takatà was created in 1914 by the Club Natació Atlètic-Barceloneta (CNAB) swimmers as part of their winter training for when the sea was rough. The CNAB didn't have indoor pools yet, so this sport did the trick. It's halfway between beach volleyball and tennis, played in pairs, using hands and a tennis ball. Rules: players have to hit the ball once and send it over the net in an ascending trajectory; they can't shoot it down or hold it. Scoring is to 40 points in friendly matches and to 60 in official ones. There is no federation or sports clubs dedicated to *takatà*, but the CNAB has spaces on the beach to play it.

Homage to the Swimmers

The love story between Barceloneta neighbourhood and water sports has existed since 1913, when the first local swimming and water polo clubs were founded. In Plaça del Mar, you'll spot the **Homenatge a la natació** steel sculpture designed by Alfredo Lanz in 2004.

KAPRIK/GETTY IMAGES ©

Barcelona (Moll de la Marina s/n) you'll find **Supyoga Catalunya** School. It organises daily sunrise and sunset lessons at Somorrostro beach as well as in different Costa Brava spots.

No pain, no gain Brave Barceloneta is also into winter sea swimming, so it's easy to spot swimmers of all ages all year round, especially in the early-morning hours. On 1 January at noon, Club Natació Atlètic-Barceloneta greets the arrival of the new year by organising a massive swim on Sant Sebastià beach. Called **Primer Bany de l'Any** (First Swim of the Year) and practised since 1996, it attracts more than 400 fearless swimmers. Online registration is required to join and the largely symbolic fee is always donated to solidarity causes.

FAR LEFT: VICTOR SANTACRUZ/SHUTTERSTOCK © LEFT: SOPA IMAGES/GETTY IMAGES ©

Left Surfers on Barceloneta beach **Top** *Homenatge a la natació* sculpture by Alfredo Lanz **Above** Swimming at Barceloneta beach

16 Maritime CULTURE

SEAFOOD | HERITAGE TOURS | SUSTAINABILITY

Tucked between the Aquàrium and Sant Sebastià beach lies **Moll dels Pescadors**, the city's fishing dock. Unnoticed by many *barcelonins*, it's here that fresh fish caught in nearby waters are unloaded, weighed and auctioned from Monday to Friday. As in many other cities, Barcelona's fishing activity seems to be slowly drowning, but Barceloneta keeps its maritime history alive.

How to

Getting here Barceloneta metro station is the easiest way to get to the neighbourhood.

When to go Fishing-themed tours around the dock run from Monday to Friday. If you're planning to go on a seafood-tapas crawl around the neighbourhood, keep in mind that most bars and restaurants are very busy on the weekends and closed on Mondays.

Fresh catch Peixateria Montse i Jesús is the only stall in Barceloneta's market that sells fish from the city's fish market.

Boat-to-Table Tours

Have you ever wondered what happens between the moment a fish is caught and its arrival on your plate? Do you know how to become a more conscious fish consumer? Anna Bozzano and Arianna Bucci from **El peix al plat** and Cristina Caparrós from **Capamar** have the answers to these questions. Both companies offer highly recommended organised and tailor-made marine experiences, visits to the local dock and the fish-market auction, kid-friendly activities, fishing day-trips, tastings, cooking classes and sustainability workshops focused on Barcelona's fishing sector and culture.

El peix al plat Anna and Arianna are two über-friendly

Top right Fishing from a Barceloneta pier **Right** Torre del Rellotge clock tower

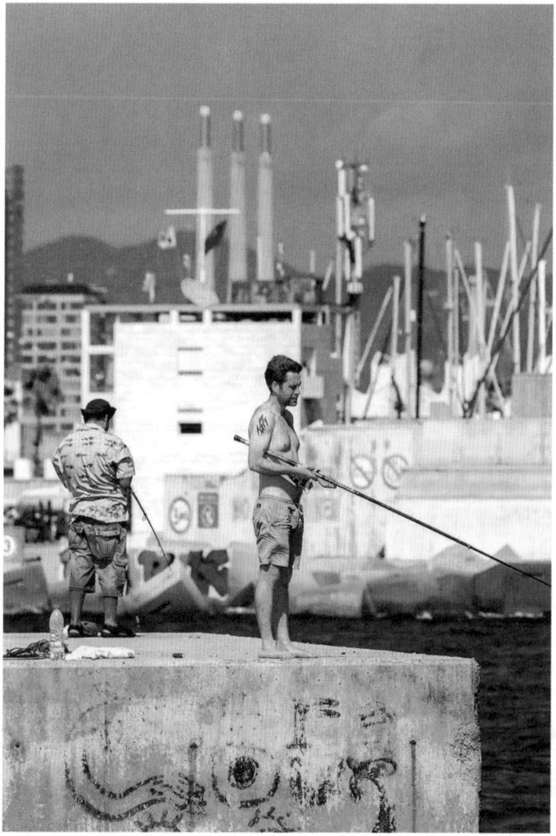

KAVALENKAU/SHUTTERSTOCK ©

BILL PERRY/SHUTTERSTOCK ©

Eat Local Fish

Some restaurants serving fish and seafood from Barcelona's fish market:

La Mar Salada (Passeig de Joan de Borbó 58)

Can Ros (Carrer de l'Almirall Aixada 7)

1881 Sagardi (Plaça de Pau Vila 3)

Can Ramonet (Carrer de la Maquinista 17)

Italian-born women with doctorates in marine biology who one day decided to replace scientific research at the desk with scientific outreach on the dock. Currently in charge of Barcelona's fishermen's guild's tourist visits, their tours embark on a maritime journey filled with down-to-earth scientific explanations mixed with city secrets. Find them at linktr.ee/Elpeixalplat.

Capamar Born and bred in Barceloneta, seawater runs through Cristina Caparrós' veins. She's the daughter, granddaughter and great-granddaughter of fishermen and quit her professional career in biotechnology to transform the shrinking family trade into a successful direct-to-consumer fish business – laplatjeta.net. Along with other local families, she also founded Capamar (capamarbcn.com), a tourism company whose goal is to promote the *barrio* fishing culture among locals and visitors.

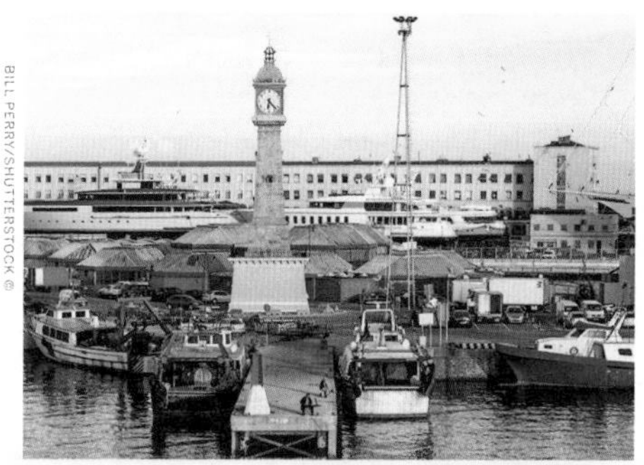

Barceloneta's Ties to the **SEA**

02

01

03

01 Torre del Rellotge
This former lighthouse, built in 1772 and transformed into a clock tower, is a beloved local landmark.

02 Maritime street name
Carrer del Mar (sea), dels Pescadors (fishermen), de l'Atlàntida (Atlantis) and dels Mariners (sailors) evidence the area's bond with the sea.

03 Mare de Déu del Carme procession
On 16 July, Barceloneta honours the patron saint of seafarers, Mare de Déu del Carme. A painted wooden sculpture of her image is carried by her devotees.

04 Facultat Nàutica de Barcelona
What better spot to have the city's nautical authority than in this neighbourhood?'

05 Ceramic wall tiles

Some street walls are decorated with sea-themed ceramic tiles; fishermen, boats, nets and seafood still lifes.

06 Barceloneta's flag

Blue for the sea, yellow for the sand and a central shield with a boat and the Torre del Rellotge. Designed by Francisco López, a local man.

07 Frank Ghery's Peix sculpture

This impressive, copper-hued, stain-less-steel, fish-shaped sculpture at the foot of the deluxe Hotel Arts Barcelona sparkles magically at sunset.

01 JOINTSTAR/SHUTTERSTOCK ©, **02** LOBROART/SHUTTERSTOCK ©, **03** 1APIX/ALAMY STOCK PHOTO ©, **04** AGEFOTOSTOCK/ALAMY STOCK PHOTO ©, **05** PETER HORREE/ ALAMY STOCK PHOTO © **06** GOGA18128/SHUTTERSTOCK ©, **07** NITO/SHUTTERSTOCK ©

17 Behind BORBÓ

WALKING | HISTORY | FOOD & DRINK

Luckily for Barceloneta's residents, most visitors venturing here only stroll down Passeig de Joan de Borbó to chill on the beaches. But behind this over-touristy promenade, you'll encounter charming little squares, a baroque church, the local market, timeworn bars, colourful facades covered with laundry drying in the sea breeze, and elders pulling chairs onto the streets to gossip when the summer heat subsides.

NITO/SHUTTERSTOCK ©

How to

Getting here Get off at Barceloneta metro station. Easy-peasy.

When to go Most bars and restaurants are closed on Monday; the area gets particularly packed in summer.

Flag raising Barceloneta is the only neighbourhood in the city where its own flag (blue and yellow with a shield in the middle) waves from more balconies than the pro-Catalan-independence flag (yellow and red stripes with a white five-pointed star).

JUAN BAUTISTA/ALAMY STOCK PHOTO ©

Get Lost in Barceloneta

Passeig de Joan de Borbó's tacky souvenir shops, international fast food chains, kebab joints and pre-cooked, defrosted paella restaurants seem to work as a contingency wall to keep alive the spirit of this atmospheric 18th-century neighbourhood of tight-knit gridded streets with a rich industrial and fishing heritage and strong working-class pride.

Wander around The best way to enjoy the city's smallest barrio is to get lost in it. Therefore, switch on your flâneur mode. Start off in **Baluard** bakery (Carrer del Baluard 38) and get yourself a delicious French-style pastry to snack on while you wander around the area. Eventually, you'll bump into attention-grabbing buildings such as the **Mercat de la Barceloneta** (Plaça del Poeta Boscà 1), the Modernista **Cooperativa La Fraternitat** public library (Carrer del Comte de Santa Clara 8), the historical research centre **Casa de la Barceloneta 1761** (Carrer de Sant Carles 6) and the former gas factory turned into an environmental education centre **La Fàbrica del Sol** (Passeig de Salvat Papasseït 1). In between these places, you might also stumble across reminders of the neighbourhood's industrial past, like **La Maquinista Terrestre y Marítima** metallurgical factory's original archway.

Settle in Dry mouth? Find vermouth in **Bar Electricitat** (Carrer de Sant Carles 15) and **Lokillo** (Carrer del Mar 75); beer in **Vaso de Oro** (Carrer de Balboa 6) and **Bodega Fermín** (Carrer de Sant Carles 18); and wine in **La Vinoteca** (Carrer de la Maquinista 14) and **La Violeta** (Carrer del Baluard 58).

Left Mercat de la Barceloneta **Bottom left** Cooperativa La Fraternitat library

Bombs for Foodies

Yep, Barceloneta is a seafood heaven for many locals, but its only contribution to Catalan cuisine has nothing to do with salty waters. It's called bomba (bomb in English) and it's a deep-fried breaded ball made of mashed potatoes with minced pork inside and served with aioli and a spicier cayenne-based sauce. Try it at La Cova Fumada (Carrer del Baluard 56).

18 Barcelona's BROOKLYN

WALKING | ART & DESIGN | FOOD & DRINK

This former working-class industrial *barrio,* filled with warehouses and former factories, has changed drastically over the last two decades. The human landscape features elderly residents pushing shopping trolleys, hipsters on fixie bikes, artists, designers, students, clubbers, gig goers and craft-beer junkies. The menu features everything from flat whites to *cafés con leche,* tacos to tapas.

JOAN_BAUTISTA/SHUTTERSTOCK ©

How to

Getting here & around Get off at Bogatell, Llacuna or Poblenou metro stations and go with the flow on foot.

Art agenda poblenouurbandistrict.com keeps track of local exhibitions and events.

Brunch o'clock Little Fern (Carrer de Pere IV 168), Espai Joliu (Carrer de Badajoz 95), Can Dendê (Carrer de la Ciutat de Granada 44), Frutas Selectas (Carrer de Pujades 95) and the Cake Man (Carrer de l'Amistat 18) will start the day off well.

JOAN_BAUTISTA/SHUTTERSTOCK ©

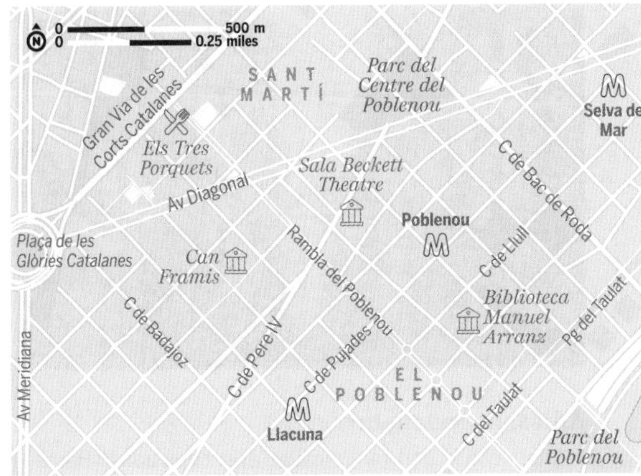

Industrial Past Recycled

Far from disowning its past, **Poblenou** flaunts it; many public facilities and private businesses are located in former factories and workshops. Wet your whistle and grab a few bites while exploring this up-and-coming area of the city.

Below the skyscraper-high-tech 22@ innovation district, there's **Sala Beckett** theatre (Carrer de Pere IV 228), a former workers' cooperative. The worth-a-visit bar **El Menjador** is on its ground floor. Just a block away is **Can Felipa** community centre (Carrer de Pallars 277), once a cotton bleaching company. A bit further down, you'll encounter **Biblioteca Manuel Arranz** public library (Carrer del Joncar 35), a former fabric printer. Ice-cream cravings? Head to **Cosi Doci** (Carrer de Pujades 218). Cocktail thirst? **Balius** (Carrer de Pujades, 196) is the answer.

Going west, Poblenou's most famous nightclub, **Razzmatazz** (Carrer dels Almogàvers 122), was once a motorcycle manufacturer, and an erstwhile boiler workshop is now **L'Ovella Negra Marina** (Carrer de Zamora 78), a temple to beer today.

In the neighbourhood's southern part, the now-disappeared flour production company **Can Gili Nou** (Carrer del Taulat 3) became the current senior social centre. The popular chamfered bar **El Santet** (Avinguda d'Icària 215) is a stone's throw away.

Industry overloaded? Stroll down the charming tree-lined Rambla de Poblenou. **Els tres porquets** (No 165), **Can Recasens** (No 102), **Monopol** (No 74) and **El 58** (No 58) can satisfy your hunger. The tiger-nut milkshake shop **Horchatería Tío Che** (No 44) will quench your thirst.

Left A Poblenou streetscape
Bottom left Sala Beckett theatre

Artists, Designers & Property Sharks

In the early 2000s, Poblenou's disused industrial space was a crowd-puller for artists, designers and the like. Unsurprisingly, art studios, galleries and schools mushroomed here overnight. Good news: the *barrio* has become an indisputable creative epicentre. **Can Framis** Contemporary Painting Museum (fundaciovilacasas.com), **La Plataforma** (laplataformabcn.com) and **Dada Studios** (dada-studios.com) galleries, **BAU Design College** (baued.es), **Roc 35** gastronomic workshop (roc35.com), **BD Barcelona** design studio (bdbarcelona.com) as well as **Palo Alto** (es.paloalto.barcelona) and **La Escocesa** (laescocesa.org) creative hubs are the proof. Bad news: the area has also turned into a housing-speculation hotspot.

Wave of Gentrification

TOURISTS, GO HOME

For over two decades now, Barceloneta's characteristic outdoor ceramic wall tiles illustrating virgins, saints, patrons and old traditions have been sharing space with furious graffiti ordering tourists to go back to where they came from. But why?

KIKOKBP/SHUTTERSTOCK ©

Left Barceloneta buildings **Middle** Barceloneta residents **Right** A calm residential street

Adiós, Barceloneta?

Touristification and gentrification are not unique to Barcelona nor to this 1.3-sq-km *barrio* that houses 15,000 neighbours, but considering its rather minuscule size and many of the locals' socio-economic profile, it's undoubtedly the neighbourhood that has suffered the biggest impact.

Twenty-eight sq metres is the total surface of a good number of apartments in the Barceloneta, the so-called *quarts de casa*. These were built in the 18th and 19th centuries to house migrants who moved to the neighbourhood to work in the booming industrial and fishing sectors. A century later, these working-class buildings would become a magnet for eager real-estate investors willing to turn them into tourist rental apartments and foreigners' second homes. Rents climbed up, local amenities became souvenir shops and fast-food chains, and beaches started attracting unwanted boozy and noisy night crowds. Neighbours were being displaced from their homes and public spaces, but they soon took action. Hundreds of demonstrations and endless meetings with the city council have been organised by various neighbourhood associations and local entities to fight against this global economic tsunami that erodes away life-long residents and cultural identity. These associations and entities, combined with the residents' strong sense of belonging, have managed to pause and even overthrow unfair urban plans that involved eviction among other predatory actions. However, a lot of damage has already been done. Hence the graffiti.

Do Barcelonins Hate Tourists?

It's more of a love-hate relationship and it all comes down to numbers. Their city has one of the highest population

MARTIN HUGHES/LONELY PLANET ©

TASSOS MARINITSIS/SHUTTERSTOCK ©

densities in Europe; 1.6 million inhabitants live in a 100 sq km area that relies heavily on the tourism sector, which makes up 15% of its GDP. In 2019, Barcelona received 12 million visitors. When COVID-19 swiped them away, locals reclaimed its centre and other spots that had been engulfed by mass tourism since the city hosted the 1992 Summer Olympics. Simultaneously, the local unemployment rate went up and hundreds of businesses shut down. Just like pre-pandemic times, the city government juggles citizens' needs with the consequences of an economic monoculture overly focused on tourism. Everything suggests that in the post-pandemic era, rebalancing the relationship between *barcelonins* and visitors will continue to be one of the city council's toughest challenges.

> Neighbours were being displaced from their homes and public spaces, but they soon took action.

How to Be a Responsible Visitor

Avoid booking tourist rental apartments and stay in a hotel whenever possible. If you're travelling on a limited budget, book a room in a neighbourhood hotel. They tend to be cheaper than the ones located in central and touristy areas. Staying in a traditional B&B or guesthouse is also a great way to support the local economy. Before booking any accommodation, go to the city council's fairtourism.barcelona website to check if it's licensed. Try to travel in the low season; it helps spread accommodation demand. Finally, shop and eat local. Independently owned businesses: do. International chains: don't.

Common-Sense Etiquette Required

When in Barcelona, just like in any other place in the world, behave as if you were visiting your in-laws for the first time. No shirtless outfits, no boozed-up street performances, no public urination, no unsolicited photos. Stand on the right of the metro escalators and use the litter bins (preferably, the recycling ones). Markets are not photoshoot backgrounds; buy seasonal unpackaged stuff and not ready-cut fruits sold for tourists. Finally, practise the four magic words (*hola*, *adéu*, *per favor*, *gràcies* in Catalan and *hola*, *adiós*, *por favor*, *gracias* in Spanish). Your in-laws' house is not a theme park, and neither is Barcelona. Remember: like people, cities are vulnerable and unique.

Listings

BEST OF THE REST

Timeworn & Newcomer Restaurants

Els Pescadors €€€

Tucked in the seaside-village-vibe Plaça Prim square, this elegant family-run restaurant offers superb rice dishes and fresh fish from the best Catalan fish markets.

Xiringuito Escribà €€€

The Escribà family, a famous four-generation *barcelonin* pastry dynasty, nails paellas and *fideuàs* just like chocolate cakes and tartes tatin. Kitchen service at this popular waterfront restaurant runs all day.

Can Solé €€€

The oldest restaurant in Barceloneta. Its white-jacketed waiters have served freshly caught seafood and rice dishes to the cream of Spanish society, from Joan Miró to Rafael Nadal. Try the *sarsuela*, a traditional Valencian and Catalan seafood and fish casserole. Opposite Barceloneta's market.

Green Spot €€

One of the best vegetarian restaurants in Spain, its slogan is 'veggies for veggies and non-veggies'. Veggie-sceptical tested international dishes, from curry to quesadillas. Nordic ambience and outdoor seating available. Close-by Barceloneta metro station.

NAP Mar €

NAP stands for Neapolitan Authentic Pizza and *mar* means sea in Catalan and Spanish. It's crystal clear; traditional Naples-style pizzas a stone's throw from Barceloneta beach.

Doroteo BCN €

Tacos, Mexican beers and tempting funky cocktails. On warm nights, try for a table in the charming little square and enjoy Poblenou life passing by. Next to Can Felipa.

Hip Bars, Old Boozers & Craft Beer Sanctuaries

Camping €

Right next to Parc del Poblenou's basketball courts there's a small outdoor box-shaped bar with 10 wooden tables filled with hipsters. All taken? The grass is yours. Weekly pop-up food events.

Van Van VAR €

This 14-sq-metre bar with a welcoming sunny terrace is managed by a food-truck company. New nibbles every week. Short walking distance from Parc de la Ciutadella.

Perikete €

The 200 wine varieties sold by the glass or bottle and the 50 different tapas attract crowds to this bustling bar. Behind Port Vell.

Can Paixano Barceloneta €

You might need to elbow your way into this cramped old-school bar, but the rosé *cava* (sparkling wine) and the bite-sized meat *bocadillos* (filled rolls) are worth it. Near Barceloneta metro station.

La Pubilla del Taulat €

This bar around the corner from Poblenou's market has served homemade tapas and excellent wine to a loyal following since 1886.

Hoppiness €

Not far from Poblenou cemetery, this laid-back corner bar with an outdoor terrace has 12 taps with rotating local craft beers. Sandwiches, burgers and a DJ spinning vinyl on Saturday afternoons.

La Cervecita €

Craft beer bar and shop with 17 taps and more than 200 bottles from various countries. The owners are the neighbourhood's beer festival organisers. One step away from Rambla de Poblenou.

Freddo Fox €

Around the corner from Bogatell metro station, two Americans with heaps of brewing experience and numerous awards manage this outstanding craft beer shop and brewery. Opens 4pm to 8pm Wednesday to Friday.

La Cervesera de Poblenou €

The city's first brewery that produces exclusively organic craft beers. Tastings are on Friday at 7.30pm. Booking ahead is necessary. Located close to Glòries metro station.

Books, Vinyl & Local Fashion Design

Nollegiu

A former '50s fashion boutique turned into a well-stocked bookshop. The district's unofficial cultural embassy. Books in Catalan, Spanish and English. A short hop away from Poblenou market.

Ultra-Local Records

Very close to Llacuna metro station, this well-curated shop sells secondhand Catalan, Spanish, French, British and American records.

System Action Outlet

Poblenou's most famous women's fashion brand. Casual and urban clothing, accessories and shoes. It has 20 shops around Spain. Two blocks away from Llacuna metro station.

FOTOKON/SHUTTERSTOCK©

Cementiri de Poblenou

Art Attack

Museu del Disseny de Barcelona

The city's design museum houses a sensational collection of ceramics, textiles, decorative and graphic arts. A must for design-world enthusiasts. Adjacent to Jean Nouvel's Torre Glòries.

Fundació KBr MAPFRE Barcelona Photo Center

Named Kbr as a homage to the potassium bromide used in the developing process, this new 1400-sq-metre photo exhibition centre is located at the foot of Torre MAPFRE.

Mausoleums, Sculptures & Legends

Cementiri de Poblenou

Inland from Platja de Bogatell, the local cemetery houses tombs of eminent and anonymous Catalans like Santet de Poblenou, a venerated 22-year-old said to have had supernatural powers, who passed away in 1899.

LA SAGRADA FAMÍLIA & L'EIXAMPLE

ARCHITECTURE & CULTURE | SHOPPING | FOOD & DRINK

LA SAGRADA FAMÍLIA & L'EIXAMPLE
Trip Builder

TAKE YOUR PICK OF MUST-SEES AND HIDDEN GEMS

L'Eixample is much more than its Modernista landmarks. With one foot firmly planted in its bourgeois past and another in the cutting-edge present and future, the old and the new are two amicable neighbours who cohabit in total harmony in this always-evolving district.

Neighbourhood Notes

Best for Modernista architecture, contemporary art, fashion shopping, local and international fare, casual craft beers and refined cocktails.

Transport The area boasts 20 metro stations.

Getting around Make the most of the district's wide sidewalks and discover it on foot.

Tip Lift your gaze up when strolling in L'Eixample to seek out mind-blowing building facades.

Shop guilt-free for local fashion around **Passeig de Gràcia** and Rambla de Catalunya.
Maximum 12 mins from Passeig de Gràcia metro station

Poke your nose into non-Modernista art in **Marlborough Barcelona**.
5 mins from Diagonal metro station

Mercat del Ninot

Hospital Clínic

Use the eye-catching chamfered corner at **Casa Ferran Guardiola – Casa Xina** as the perfect background for your selfies.
5 min from Universitat metro station

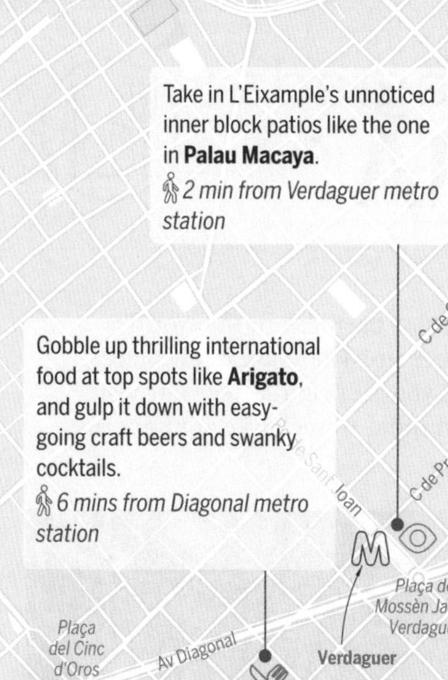

Take in L'Eixample's unnoticed inner block patios like the one in **Palau Macaya**.
2 min from Verdaguer metro station

Pick through bric-à-brac, antiques and secondhand clothing in **Mercat dels Encants**.
1 min from Glòries metro station

Gobble up thrilling international food at top spots like **Arigato**, and gulp it down with easy-going craft beers and swanky cocktails.
6 mins from Diagonal metro station

Mingle with *barcelonins* in their natural shopping state in **Mercat de la Concepció**.
1 min from Girona metro station

Get bookish and cosy in **Llibreria Finestres** bookstore.
4 min from Passeig de Gràcia metro station

Add to the throng in **Gaixample** after dark.
Maximum 8 mins from Universitat metro station

19 After La Sagrada FAMÍLIA

FOOD | DRINKS | PEACE & QUIET

Overwhelmed by one of the most spectacular basilicas in the world? Tourist throngs running down your energy? Cheer up! There are a few places around La Sagrada Família where you can treat yourself right after your visit. Something to nibble or sip, and some peace and quiet to recharge your energy.

VTT STUDIO/SHUTTERSTOCK ©

How to

Getting here & around Jump off at Sagrada Família metro station and set off on foot to find out what the area can offer you besides the basilica.

When to go It's lively all year round. Mind you, shops and some bars and restaurants close on Sundays.

Brewed history Estrella Damm is one of the best-selling beer brands in Spain. Visits to Estrella Damm Old Brewery (Carrer de Rosselló 515), founded by an Alsatian brewer in 1876, include tastings.

XAVI LAPUENTE/SHUTTERSTOCK ©

Nibbles Head to **Xurreria Sagrada Familia** (Plaça de la Sagrada Família 26) for irresistible churros covered in sugar and dipped in hot chocolate and to **Carambola** (Carrer de Lepant 269) for traditional and not-so-traditional artisan ice creams. Hungrier? In **Can Pizza** (Passatge de Simó 21) you'll find good pizzas in a funky venue with roof windows overlooking the basilica's towers. Go veggie in **Green & Burger** (Plaça de la Sagrada Família 3), go full-on meaty in **Bardeni el Meatbar** (Carrer de València 454), go Mex in **La Taquería** (Passatge de Font 5) and go Castilian in **Hasta los Andares** (Carrer de Provença 471), a Manchegan tavern serving flavoursome cured hams, cold cuts and cheeses.

Sips Vermouth buffs will be in heaven at **Bodega El Sidral** (Carrer Dos de Maig 213), a neighbourly hidden gem that also serves salted anchovies to die for. Old-hat **Bodega Celler Miquel** (Carrer de Castillejos 345) is an excellent option for unpretentious wine and *cava* connoisseurs; craft beer aficionados should head to **La Cerveseria Clandestina** (Carrer de Còrsega 611).

Peace Loosen up at the rooftop bar of **Ayre Hotel Rosselló** (Carrer de Rosselló 390) while enjoying deluxe cocktails and views. Afraid of heights? Stay grounded in **Jardins Beatriu de Provença** (Carrer de Nàpols 244) or **Jardins d'Enriqueta Sèculi** (Passatge de Simó 15), with hidden inner block patios.

Left Alfresco dining with La Sagrada Família in the background
Bottom left Estrella Damm beer

Overlooked Passages

Barcelona has 400 passages and most of them remain unnoticed even by locals. In the Sagrada Família area, **passatge de León** and **passatge de Pau Hernández** are connected to form a triangle, an absolute rarity. The humble houses built here were intended for working-class people who moved to the city during its booming industrial years in the early 1900s.

Gaudí Behind Closed Doors

TALK ABOUT GAUDÍ AS IF YOU WERE HIS GREAT-GREAT-GRANDCHILD

By now you may know that Catalan's most famous architect was born into a line of coppersmiths, and about the influence nature had on his work. You've probably heard about his solid religious faith and the streetcar incident that caused his death. But what about his early years, his love life and his diet?

Left Gaudí c. 1882 **Middle** Gaudí c. 1888 **Right** La Sagrada Família

Baby Antoni

Gaudí's exact birthplace remains uncertain. Some say he was born in 1852 in the town of Reus (Tarragona province) and others in his family's summer house, in Riudoms village (6km from Reus).

However, there is consensus on his physical appearance – he was nothing like the Spanish stereotype. The architect had Nordic features, blond hair, pale skin and blue eyes.

Young Antoni

Aged 18, Gaudí moved from Reus to Barcelona to pursue his academic career in architecture. Far from being a top-class student, when he finally got his degree the architecture school's headmaster allegedly said, 'Who knows if we have given a diploma to a madman or a genius? Time will tell'.

The newly graduated architect's earliest works in Barcelona involved designing Plaça Reial's public lighting lampposts, a display case for a glove shop in Carrer d'Avinyó and the interior of a pharmacy on Passeig de Gràcia.

Single Antoni

It's believed that Gaudí fell in love only once in his life. The woman in question was Pepeta Moreu, a worker-cooperative teacher from Mataró. His feelings were not reciprocated and he never got married. Nobody knows if his celibacy was based on religion or if it was a consequence of his one failed marriage proposal to Pepeta, but rumour has it that he probably died a virgin. His niece Rosa Egea once stated that her uncle was not interested in women.

APIC/GETTY IMAGES ©

YINGNA CAI/SHUTTERSTOCK ©

Political Antoni

Despite being a fervent Catalan patriot, Gaudí always refused to run whenever local politicians asked him to get politically involved in Catalonia's fight for autonomy.

On 11 September 1920, during Catalonia's National Day celebrations, he got beaten up by the police in a small street riot that took place in the Jocs Florals, a Catalan poetry contest with floral prizes. Four years later on that very same day, he was arrested for speaking in Catalan to a policeman. He had broken the dictator Primo de Rivera's ban on the language and was put in a cell for four hours until La Mercè's church rector paid his 50-peseta bail.

Four years later... he was arrested for speaking in Catalan to a policeman.

Veggie Antoni

The architect suffered from poor health from an early age, mainly rheumatism. In his teen years and along with his father, he became a strict vegetarian when almost nobody in Catalonia was, and adopted some of the early naturopathic and hydrotherapy principles of Dr Sebastian Kneipp. As an adult, he would only eat vegetables, fruit, nuts, olive oil, bread and honey, and drink tiny amounts of water. No coffee, no alcohol, no meat nor fish for him. By the end of his life, when he was a flat-broke architect who had to go door to door asking for donations to finish La Sagrada Família, he subsisted on lettuce leaves sprinkled with olive oil and nuts. Gaudí also practised fasting regularly, and he always refused any professional medical advice on his self-invented diet.

Antoni's Biggest Fan

Salvador Dalí always expressed his veneration for Gaudí's audacious buildings and was one of the first avant-garde artists to publicly praise him. In fact, the painter's obsession with the architect and his influence is present throughout his pictorial work, from *Dionysus Spitting the Complete Image of Cadaqués on the Tip of the Tongue of a Three-Storied Gaudinian Woman* (1958) to *Double Victory of Gaudí* (1982). The surrealist artist believed that a talent like Gaudí wouldn't be seen again for centuries. No surprises here; both geniuses rejected realism's traditional rules and were gifted with a unique sensitivity.

20 L'Eixample's Hidden PATIOS

WALKING | URBAN OASES | FOOD

There are close to 80 urban oases scattered throughout Barcelona that go largely unnoticed by most visitors. These include stunning backyards, luscious gardens, lively playgrounds, architectural gems, benches where you can sit under the shade of a tree with a view of local life. Inhale tranquillity, exhale urban stress.

EQROY/SHUTTERSTOCK ©

How to

Getting here & around L'Eixample has 20 metro stations; check the nearest one to your destination beforehand.

When to go Most inner patios are open 10am to 7pm during autumn and winter and 10pm to 9pm during spring and summer.

Recognising women With the aim of feminising Barcelona's nomenclature, which is almost monopolised by male figures, the city's council has named many inner patios after eminent women.

EQROY/SHUTTERSTOCK ©

Behind Universitat de Barcelona's building the **Jardins Ferran Soldevila** (Gran Via de les Corts Catalanes 585) is a garden with over 150 plant species of ancient trees, ponds and a greenhouse; it's an oasis of wisdom and nature open to everyone. Grab a coffee beforehand in the nearby **Vascobelo V-bar**. The one that serves the uni's canteen is as forgettable as your most mediocre college teacher.

The neoclassical **Jardí del Palau Robert** (Passeig de Gràcia 107) was built in 1898 as an aristocrat's private residence. It's currently Catalonia's regional tourist office and an exhibition space. In the back, there's a palm-tree garden that is sometimes used for outdoor exhibitions and concerts. Within reach and behind a wooden door, you'll find **Les Filles Cafè**; a cute front yard with a terrace, stylwish indoors and organic food.

ELENA MANSUROVA/SHUTTERSTOCK ©

Seu de l'Editorial Gustavo Gili

Hidden in an inner block patio, designed by Grup R and built in 1954, Gustavo Gili's former publishing house headquarters (Carrer de Rosselló 87–89) is an example of Barcelona's often undervalued modern architectural heritage. This rationalist building reflects the influence of the GATCPAC, Frank Lloyd Wright and the Bauhaus School.

Top left, above Jardí del Palau Robert
Left Torre de les Aigües

Named after a famous Catalan soprano and opened in 2016, **Jardí de Montserrat Figueras** (Carrer de Còrsega 195) is an inner block patio that boasts an animated kids' wooden playground. It's also a good example of how, in the mid-'80s, Barcelona's city council started reappropriating disused spaces to combat the dramatic lack of greenery. Not far away, there's the Mexican-owned **Cloudstreet Bakery**, serving organic-flour breads and terrific croissants and cinnamon rolls.

An inner block with an old 24m water tower, **Jardins de la Torre de les Aigües** (Carrer de Roger de Llúria 56) was known until recently as 'L'Eixample's beach'. The knee-high swimming pool helped the youngest barcelonins beat the heat for 40 years. Today it's no longer a usable pool, but the patio can still be visited. The charming art-deco **Passatge de Permanyer** pedestrian passage is opposite it and the light-filled Galician and Basque corner bar **Norte** is only a few steps away, with homey

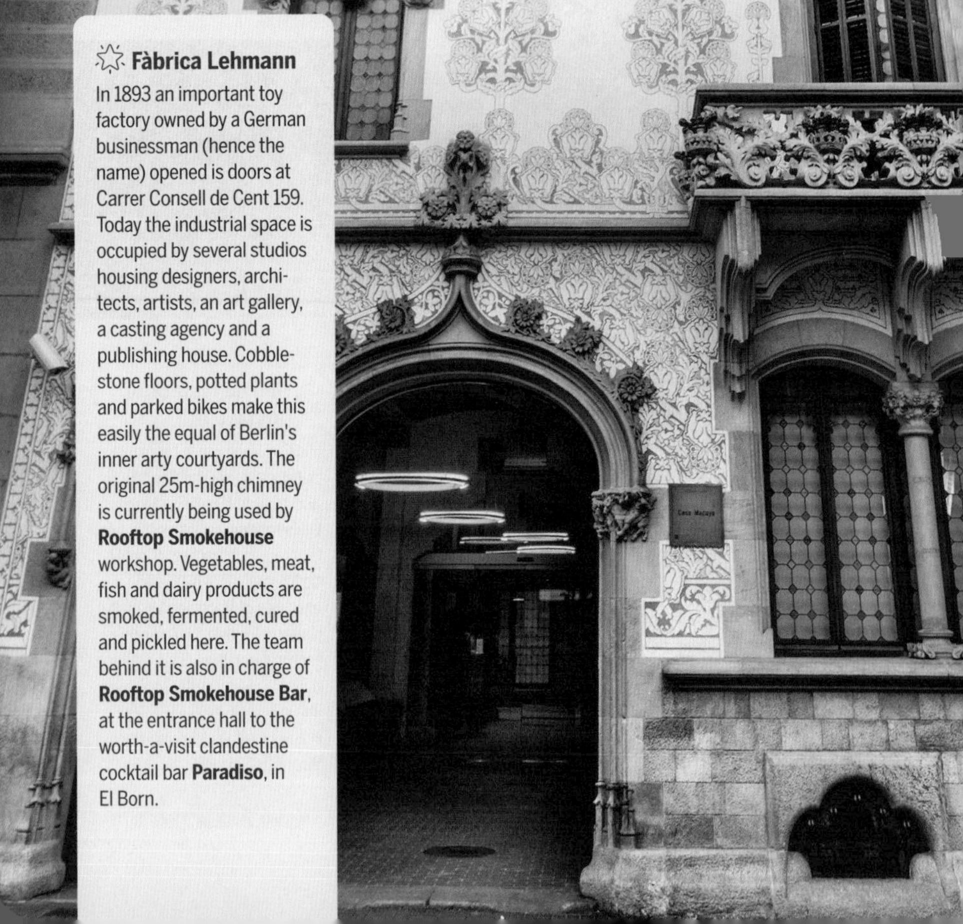

Fàbrica Lehmann

In 1893 an important toy factory owned by a German businessman (hence the name) opened is doors at Carrer Consell de Cent 159. Today the industrial space is occupied by several studios housing designers, architects, artists, an art gallery, a casting agency and a publishing house. Cobblestone floors, potted plants and parked bikes make this easily the equal of Berlin's inner arty courtyards. The original 25m-high chimney is currently being used by **Rooftop Smokehouse** workshop. Vegetables, meat, fish and dairy products are smoked, fermented, cured and pickled here. The team behind it is also in charge of **Rooftop Smokehouse Bar**, at the entrance hall to the worth-a-visit clandestine cocktail bar **Paradiso**, in El Born.

Left Palau Macaya **Below** Jardins de la Torre de les Aigües

cooking, good breakfasts, delicious tortillas (omelettes) and small producers' wines.

Attached to **Església de la Concepció** neo-Gothic church (don't miss its cloister) and tucked behind a noisy traffic-filled street, **Jardins del Rector Oliveras** (Passatge del Rector Oliveras 10) is pure bliss. There are climbing and aromatic plants, palm trees, a fountain, wooden benches, a kids' playground and views to the basilica's facade and neighbours' back windows. Head to nearby **Mercat de la Concepció** to get some nibbles.

On airy Passeig de Sant Joan, the white facade of **Palau Macaya** (Passeig de Sant Joan 108), with pseudo-Gothic sculptural ornamentation, stands out from the rest. Designed by Puig i Cadafalch in 1901, this free-access Modernista building managed by La Caixa bank and used as a conference centre has a magnificent interior courtyard, skylight and back patio with phenomenal views to its rear part. Two blocks down, there's **Granja Petitbo** with a Nordic vibe, mismatched furniture, brunch, set-lunch menus and afternoon cakes.

21 Beyond Boqueria MARKET

MARKETS | LOCAL LIFE | FOOD & DRINKS

Aside from over-visited Boqueria, there are 38 other food markets scattered throughout Barcelona that go largely unnoticed by most visitors. La Concepció and El Ninot markets are prime spots to get an insight into local market culture, sample regional products and try the array of classic dishes offered in the indoor bars, cafes and food stalls with tasting corners.

TRAVELLIFESTYLE/SHUTTERSTOCK ©

How to

Getting here For La Concepció get off at Passeig de Gràcia or Girona metro stations; for El Ninot head to Hospital Clínic metro station.

When to go La Concepció is open 8am to 9pm weekdays and 8am to 2pm Saturday; El Ninot is open 9am to 8pm Tuesday to Friday and 9am to 3pm Saturday.

Heads up! Fishmongers are closed on Monday, and opening hours vary in August.

JOAN_BAUTISTA/SHUTTERSTOCK ©

Mercat de la Concepció

Built in 1888, and popularly known as the Flower Market as it has two big flower stalls in one of the entrances, the impressive iron structure and large glass windows at La Concepció (Carrer d'Aragó 313–317) were inspired by Paris' Les Halles Market and London's Crystal Palace.

Foodie spots Finest olive oils from the Garrigues region, Catalonia's production epicentre, are sold at **Garrigues colors i emocions**, along with Costers del Segre wines. This lesser-known Catalan wine region is easily the equal of more well-known areas such as Priorat or Penedès. Pick up prime-quality artisan dairy products and charcuterie produced in Catalonia at **Tantdebo**; and try the prize-winning Mas El Garet cheese range.

Mercat del Ninot

Dating back to the late 19th century, El Ninot (Carrer de Mallorca 133) feels refreshingly new after its massive 2015 renovation works. The original entrance and the building's signature metal structure were kept to preserve its authentic spirit, and cool modern touches like the wavy facades were gracefully added.

Foodie hotspots Owned by a century-old, codfish-selling family dynasty, **Bacallaneria Perelló** has a spacious tasting corner serving the most traditional of Catalan cuisine's cod recipes. Buy certified Asturian, Galician, Leonese, Swiss and French premium meats at **De Cruz Morales**, have them cooked in the back kitchen and devour them at the tables.

Left A bakery in Mercat de la Concepció
Bottom left Mercat del Ninot

New Old Markets

As a result of hosting the 1992 Olympic Games, Barcelona City Council launched an ambitious market remodelling plan. It was focused on restoring the buildings, improving the waste-management systems, extending the opening hours and building small supermarkets inside the markets, as well as promoting a new business model – half food stall, half tasting corner – offering a counter-to-table service.

International CUISINE

WORLD CUISINES | BEER | COCKTAILS

Feeling tapas-overdosed? Craving non-Catalan-Spanish food? You're in the right district, amigo. Whatever cuisine you're yearning for, this *barrio* surely has it. Top it off with local craft beers or glammed-up cocktails.

Above Ramen
Right Colombian chicken soup

How to

Getting here & around L'Eixample is the district in the city with the most metro stations and bus stops. Check the closest ones to your foodie destination before heading there.

When to go August is when the majority of bars and restaurants close for summer holidays.

Shoestring eats Most restaurants offer affordable *menús del dia* (set-lunch menus) on workdays.

Latin American & Asian Food

Non-European immigration was already a growing phenomenon before the 1992 Olympic Games, but it was afterwards that the main waves of immigrants moved to Catalonia's capital. As a result, the city now has an extremely diverse dining scene, with L'Eixample one of its epicentres.

The fastest-growing communities in Barcelona are Latin American. In a very short time, their restaurants have naturally become part of the city's landscape. Top picks are the Mexican **La Chula** (Carrer de Rosselló 483), the Colombian **Mi Tierra** (Carrer Comte d'Urgell 76), the Ecuadorian **El Ñaño Bellaterra** (Carrer de Lepant 203), the Argentinean **Milo Grill** (Carrer de Balmes 127), the Venezuelan **La Cachapera** (Carrer de Vilarroel 57) and the Peruvian **Yakumanka** (Carrer de València 207).

When it comes to other cuisines, the Lebanese **Iakni** (Carrer de Vilamarí 3), the Korean **Pocha** (Carrer de Provença 224), the Filipino **Kasarap** (Carrer de Consell de Cent 141), the Vietnamese **Vietnam Kitchen** (Carrer d'Aribau 137) and the Japanese **Kanada-Ya Ramen** (Carrer de València 240), **Arigato** (Carrer de Roger de Llúria 114) and **Sato i Tanaka** (Carrer de Bruc 79) are favourites.

Is spicy Asian food your weakness? Head to the Sichuanese **Cuina Panda** (Carrer de Viladomat 101), the Malaysian **Rasa Malaysia Halal** (Passeig de Sant Joan 179), the Thai **Petit Bangkok** (Carrer de Balmes 106), the Indian **Masala73** (Carrer de Muntaner 152) or the Pakistani **Baby Jaleby** (Gran Via de les Corts Catalanes 452). If you can't decide on your preferred Asian cuisine, set off to **Hawker 45** (Carrer de Casp 45) for a mix.

European Food

Don't miss the sophisticated *pâté en croûte* meat terrine at **Bistrot Bilou** (Carrer de Pau Claris 85), which serves classic French dishes. In the casual **Wawel Restó** (Carrer de Sicília

Craft Beer & Snacks

Brew Wild BCN (Consell de Cent 255) Pizzas

Garage Beer Co (Carrer Consell de Cent 261) *Bocadillos* (filled baguettes) and tapas

La Tèxtil (Carrer de Casp 33) Street food

BierCaB (Carrer de Muntaner 55) Tapas and burgers

Conesa Beer BCN (Carrer de Casanova 62) Tapas and *coques* (savoury baked flatbread with toppings)

La Més Petita (Carrer de Diputació 30) Cheese and cold-cut platters

Craft beer shops

Rosses i torrades (Carrer de Consell de Cent 192)

BeerStore (Carrer de Provença 495)

Lambicus (Carrer de Rocafort 9)

Cocktail Connoisseurs

Head to **Ideal Cocktail Bar** (Carrer d'Aribau 89) for a cosmopolitan. Try a gin fizz at **Solange** (Carrer d'Aribau 143) or a dry martini at **Dry Martini** (Carrer d'Aribau 162). Sample white truffle pisco sours at the **Alchemix** (Carrer de València 212), or kukumbrowas at **Milano Jazz Club** (Ronda de la Universitat 35).

BOGDANHODA/SHUTTERSTOCK ©

330) you'll find hearty Polish soups, pierogi dumplings, beers and vodkas.

At Sicilian **Galú** (Carrer del Rosselló 290) you can choose from iconic dishes such as caponata, marsala chicken and cannoli. More laid-back, **Il Birrino** (Carrer d'Alí Bei 123) nails fresh pasta dishes and also has a well-chosen range of craft beers. If pizzas are your passion, try **Da Michele** (Consell de Cent 336) and **Parking Pizza** (Carrer de Londres 98). The former is a Neapolitan-pizza temple; cooking with imported southern Italian ingredients and a short menu. The latter is located in an open space venue with long shared tables and serves delicious wood-fired-oven pizzas.

Oporto (Carrer de Sardenya 296) cooks Portuguese staples; from Bulhão Pato–style clams, cod and octopus dishes to *francesinha* meat-and-cheese sandwiches. The Swedish **Pappa Sven** (Carrer de Vilarroel 22) can make you very happy with its generous smörgåsbord-style buffet, and the **Fish and Chips Shop** (Carrer de Rocafort 70) can satiate your Brit-food hunger in the blink of an eye.

FAR LEFT: STOCKCREATIONS/SHUTTERSTOCK ©
LEFT: CAMO24/SHUTTERSTOCK ©

Left Tapas and beer **Top** Dry martini cocktail **Above** Neapolitan pizza

23 Shop Outside THE BOX

SHOPPING | FASHION | FOOD & DRINK

Apart from the ubiquitous Loewe, Zara and Mango, there are more Spanish clothing brands worth wearing. Max out your credit card around Passeig de Gràcia and Rambla de Catalunya, the city's high-end and high-street shopping hubs, and regret having spent the money on Enric Granados' charming pedestrian-street bar terraces afterwards.

How to

Getting here & around Get off at Plaça de Catalunya, Passeig de Gràcia or Diagonal metro stations.

When to go Avoid Sundays, as shops are closed.

Bargain hunting Winter sales start on 7 January and summer sales on 1 July.

Womenswear and menswear Less is more for **Shon Mott** (Carrer de Pau Claris 157), a slow fashion brand that designs neutral-palette, timeless clothing. The same style mantra works for **Lurdes Bergadà** (Rambla de Catalunya 48). Influenced by Yoshi Yamamoto, she has been designing natural-fibre clothes with minimalistic flair for over 40 years. Fabric and material is also key for **Good Store** (Carrer de València 343), a multi-brand store that sells ethical and sustainable clothes designed by **Ecoalf** and **Suite 13**, among other vegan and eco-friendly brands.

Top right Camper shoe store
Right Carrer Enric Granados

TUPUNGATO/SHUTTERSTOCK ©

JORDIPHOTOGRAPHY/ALAMY STOCK PHOTO ©

Recharge on Enric Granados Pedestrian Street

Shopping is exhausting. Take a brunch break in **Cosmo Cafè** (No 3) or **Brunch&Cake** (No 19) or head to **DelaCrem** for Italian ice creams (No 15); **Alba Granados/Bala** (No 34) for lavish cocktails; **Robata** (No 55) for top-quality sushi, **El Filete Ruso** (No 95) for gourmet burgers and **Enriqueta** (No 107) for healthy international tapas.

Only womenswear It's all about classy geometric and colourful prints for **Dr Bloom** (Rambla de Catalunya 30) and **Ailanto** (Carrer d'Enric Granados 46). **Bimba&Lola** (Rambla de Catalunya 84) is also in love with bold colours and fun designs, while **Masscob** (Carrer de Provença 268) and **TCN** (Carrer de Rosselló 222) focus on simplicity. The former designs functional collections with a warm boho twist and the latter sexy and comfortable underwear, lingerie and swimwear.

Shoes Known worldwide, **Camper** (Rambla Catalunya 122) has edgy urban shoes. On the other extreme, **Calçats València** (Carrer de València 190) sells 200 different models of classic and affordable *espardenyes,* the iconic summer rope-soled flat shoes with cotton fabric uppers.

Selfie-Friendly

CHAMFERED CORNERS

01

04

02

03

01 Casa Terrades – Casa de les Punxes

Address: Avinguda Diagonal 420

Built: 1905

Architect: Josep Puig i Cadafalch

02 Casa Llopis Bofill

Address: Carrer de Bailén 113

Built: 1902

Architect: Antoni Maria Gallissà

03 Conservatori Municipal de Música de Barcelona

Address: Carrer de Bruc 110

Built: 1916

Architect: Antoni de Falguera i Sivilla

04 Cases Josefa Villanueva

Address: Carrer de València 312

Built: 1909

Architect: Julio María Fossas Martínez

05 Queviures Múrria gourmet shop

Address: Carrer Roger de Llúria 85

Founded: 1898

06 Palau Marcet

Address: Passeig de Gràcia 13

Built: 1887 & 1934

Architects: Tiberi Sabater Carné and Pere Domènech Roure

07 Casa Viuda Marfà

Address: Passeig de Gràcia 66

Built: 1905

Architect: Manuel Comas Thos

08 Casa Ferran Guardiola – Casa Xina

Address: Carrer de Muntaner 54

Built: 1929

Architect: Joan Guardiola Martínez

Listings

BEST OF THE REST

 Non-Modernista Art

Marlborough Barcelona
Opened in 2006, this well-established contemporary-art gallery represents Spanish art heavyweights such as Antonio López García and Soledad Sevilla, as well as younger talents like Hugo Fontela.

3 Punts Galeria
Emerging-art lovers, welcome. Come here to see young Catalan, Spanish and foreign interdisciplinary artists' energising works.

ADN Galeria
This gallery with a soft spot for socio-political issues exhibits local and international artists' rebellious and transgressive works, proving that art can also have a social function.

Galeria Mayoral
Prestigious gallery specialising in postwar Spanish artists from Eduardo Chillida and Luis Feito to Mari Chordà and Aurèlia Muñoz. Has a branch in Paris.

 Crammed Bookshelves

Come In
One of the longest-running English bookstores in town. The latest new fiction, nonfiction, children's and young adults' book releases are easily found here.

La Central Mallorca
Exquisitely stocked bookshop, mainly in Catalan and Spanish but also in English. From philosophy, history and anthropology to literature and graphic novels.

Llibreria Finestres
Around 800 sq metres filled with literature and critical thinking in Catalan, Spanish, English, French, German and Portuguese. Sofas, armchairs and a cafe with a cosy patio at the back.

Altaïr
The city's largest travel bookstore has some books in English and a quiet cafe with free wi-fi in the basement to chill after intense book browsing and map pointing.

 Bric-à-Brac Burst

Mercat dels Encants
Barcelona's main flea market. Five hundred stalls selling junk, antique furniture and secondhand clothes under a massive, modern, wavy mirror-ceiling. Closed on Tuesday, Thursday and Sunday.

 Sweet-Tooth Treats

L'Atelier Barcelona Escola i Pastisseria €
Bakery and pastry school run by young Ximena Pastor, a former pastry head chef of several Adrià brothers' restaurants. Superb classic and innovative cakes and pastries. Unmissable.

Ochiai and Kurimu €
Japanese cafe, bakery and ice cream shop. Expect queues as it's no longer the city's best-kept sweet secret. Takashi Ochiai, the owner, has won several awards for his skilful work.

La Pastisseria Barcelona €
Managed by Josep Maria Rodríguez, winner of the 2011 Coupe du Monde de la Pâtisserie, this shop sells magnificent seasonal confectionery. Vegan cakes are also available.

 Local Grub

Nairod €€€
The chef here masters the art of turning out-

dated ingredients such as offal or game into exciting new dishes referencing traditional Catalan recipes.

Gat Blau €€€

'Sustainable cuisine with gastronomic ambition' is the slogan. In short, seasonal, organic and wonderfully cooked, locally sourced ingredients. Plenty of vegan and vegetarian options.

Can Boneta €€

Quintessential Catalan staples with a personal twist. The €13 set-lunch menu offers three small tapas as starters plus a daily special (paella on Thursdays).

Entrepanes Díaz €

Marble bar and tables, veteran waiters in bow ties and vests and one of the city's best culinary tributes to the humble *bocadillo* (baguette). Mouthwatering tapas and masterfully poured beers.

Michelin-Star Feasts

Lasarte €€€

The only three-Michelin-star restaurant in 2021 Barcelona is overseen by the acclaimed Basque chef Martín Berasategui. Sophisticated food in an uber-contemporary dining space.

Angle €€€

Catalan celebrity chef Jordi Cruz received his first Michelin star at age 26. Skyrocketing since then, in this restaurant he mixes creative and traditional haute cuisine with coolness. Two Michelin stars.

Xerta €€€

Chef Fran López pays homage to his homeland, Terres de l'Ebre (southern coastal Catalonia). Scrumptious rice and seafood dishes on the menu. One Michelin star.

ANDYSAVCHENKO/SHUTTERSTOCK ©

Antiques for sale at Mercat dels Encants

Gaixample Boozy Evenings

Carita Bonita €

Eclectic lesbian crowds come here to start the night off well with cocktails. This three-storey bar has a small dance floor in the basement. Snacks, tapas and smoothies are also offered.

Plata Cocktail Bar €

Welcoming bartenders whip up lavish cocktails while the strategic corner terrace fills up with guys who want to see and be seen. Music-wise, a mix of dance and chill-out.

Candy Darling Bar €

Indie queer bar with DJ sets, art exhibitions, live music, pop-up markets and drag and burlesque shows. Casual underground vibe and friendly mixed regulars.

Punto BCN €

One of the most popular evening meeting points in Gaixample, attracting gay men and women of all ages, shapes and sizes. It has a billiard table.

Scan to find more things to do in L'Eixample online

GRÀCIA & PARK GÜELL

LOCAL LIFE | ARCHITECTURE | SUSTAINABLE SHOPPING

GRÀCIA & PARK GÜELL
Trip Builder

TAKE YOUR PICK OF MUST-SEES AND HIDDEN GEMS

Gràcia might be the most modern and progressive district, but it has always kept its traditional, Catalan, village feel. Its narrow lanes are dotted with vegan restaurants, eco-friendly shops and craft-beer bars, but also architectural gems like Casa Vicenç. Gràcia is also one of the most bustling neighbourhoods in Barcelona.

Neighbourhood Notes

Best for Local social life, bars, modernist architecture, sustainable shopping.

Transport For Vila de Gràcia, go to Fontana or Gràcia (FGC). For Parc Güell, go to Lesseps or Vallcarca.

Getting around Explore Gràcia on foot.

Tip The liveliest time in Gràcia is from 12.30pm to 3pm and 6pm to 9pm.

0 200 m
0 0.1 miles

VALLCARCA

Vallcarca

Plaça de Lesseps

Lesseps

Admire a Gaudí-designed house inspired by Hispanic Islamic art at **Casa Vicenç**.
4 mins from Fontana metro station

Av del Príncep d'Astúries

Explore a 130-year-old traditional market located in a modernist building at **Mercat de la Llibertat**.
6 mins from Fontana metro station

C d'Alfons XII

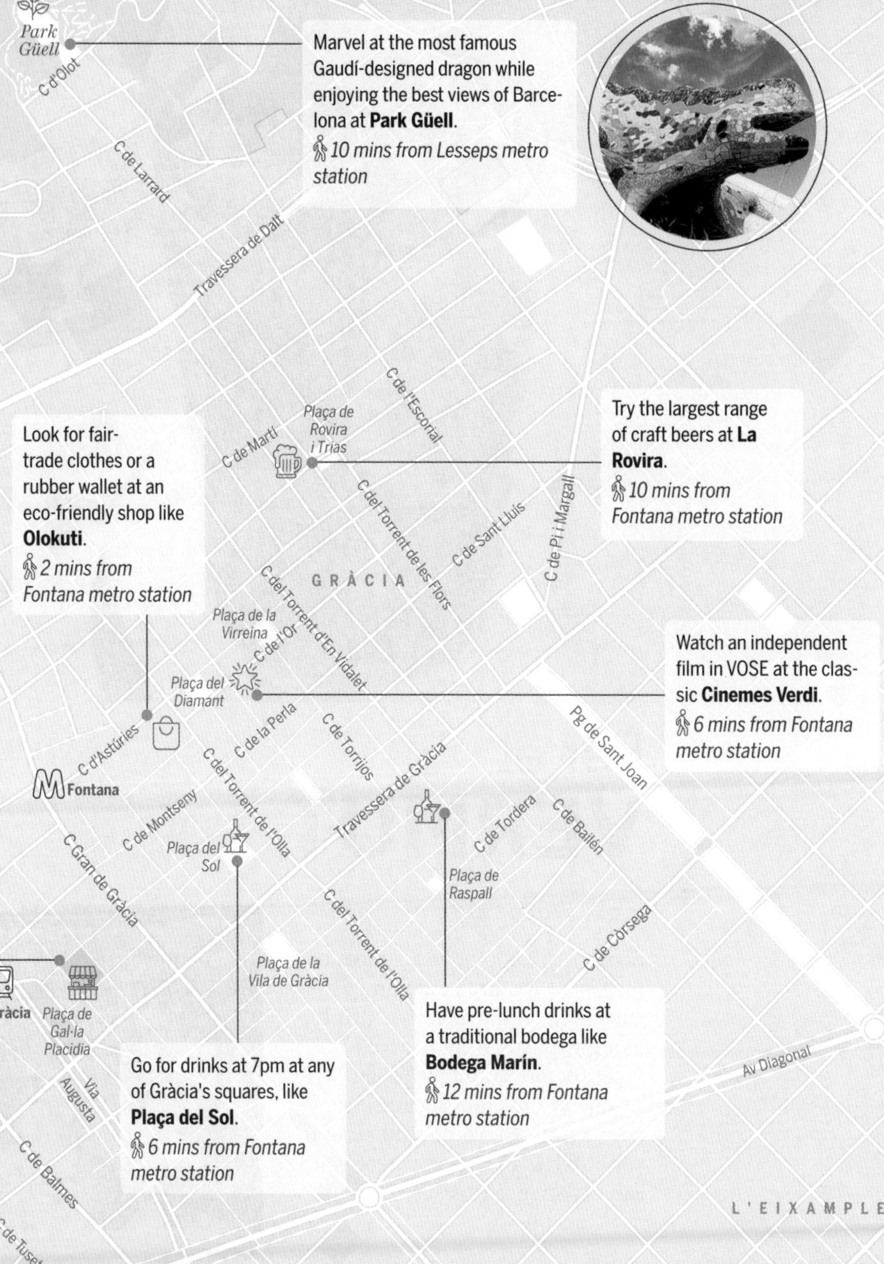
Park Güell
Marvel at the most famous Gaudí-designed dragon while enjoying the best views of Barcelona at **Park Güell**.
10 mins from Lesseps metro station
C d'Olot
C de Larrard
Travessera de Dalt
C de l'Escorial
Try the largest range of craft beers at **La Rovira**.
10 mins from Fontana metro station
Plaça de Rovira i Trias
C de Martí
Look for fair-trade clothes or a rubber wallet at an eco-friendly shop like **Olokuti**.
2 mins from Fontana metro station
C del Torrent de les Flors
C de Sant Lluís
C de Pi i Margall
GRÀCIA
C del Torrent d'En Vidalet
Plaça de la Virreina
C de l'Or
Watch an independent film in VOSE at the classic **Cinemes Verdi**.
6 mins from Fontana metro station
Plaça del Diamant
C d'Astúries
C de la Perla
C de Torrijos
Pg de Sant Joan
Fontana
C del Torrent de l'Olla
Travessera de Gràcia
C de Montseny
Plaça del Sol
C de Tordera
C de Bailén
C Gran de Gràcia
Plaça de Raspall
C del Torrent de l'Olla
C de Còrsega
Plaça de la Vila de Gràcia
Gràcia
Plaça de Gal·la Placidia
Have pre-lunch drinks at a traditional bodega like **Bodega Marín**.
12 mins from Fontana metro station
Via Augusta
Go for drinks at 7pm at any of Gràcia's squares, like **Plaça del Sol**.
6 mins from Fontana metro station
Av Diagonal
C de Balmes
C de Tuset
L'EIXAMPLE

24 Fer el VERMUT

LOCAL | FOOD | BARS

At 12.30pm, locals meet up for *fer el vermut*, a Catalan custom consisting of having a few drinks, along with some cold-served tapas, before going for lunch. As one of the main socialising points in town, you'll find several vermuteries in Gràcia where you can experience this social event.

ISAPHOTO2016/SHUTTERSTOCK ©

How to

Getting there Fontana metro station.

Average cost €1.50–3.50 for drinks; €3–6 for tapas.

When to go Every day of the year, but most locals save it for the weekend, since it involves ingesting a considerable amount of alcohol before lunch time.

Local tip On weekends, bars in Gràcia get packed, so go early (12.30pm) to find a spot, especially if you want to sit outside.

JEFFREY ISAAC GREENBERG 9+/ALAMY STOCK PHOTO ©

MARGARET STEPIEN/LONELY PLANET ©

Vermouth and fer el vermut Traditionally, the expression *fer el vermut* comes from drinking the aromatic Italian wine as an apéritif. Nowadays, it refers to the pre-lunch social meet-up, which doesn't necessarily imply drinking vermouth; you can have any drink you want. In the last couple of years, however, there seems to be a trend in which actual vermouth is coming back, and many *vermuteries* have opened in Gràcia and other parts of the city.

How to fer el vermut like the locals Keep in mind that *vermut* isn't a party, but a pretty casual event when locals socialise with their friends and family. The older people will usually start with a glass of home-made vermouth, while the youth tend to prefer a canya or a glass of wine. When it comes to food, stuffed olives and crispy chips are

Best Places in Gràcia for Vermut

La Vermu A modern *vermuteria*.

Bodega Neus Classic bodega serving since 1917

Bodega Marin The most traditional ever.

Bodega Lo Pinyol A neo-bodega. Good for *vermut*, but also at any time of the day.

Vermuteria Puigmartí Fancy tapas, with a large wine selection.

Top left A glass of *vermut* **Left** A bustling *vermuteria* **Above** *Vermut* bottles for sale

never missing from the table, always sprinkled with a local spicy sauce made of red paprika, a popular brand being Espinaler. Cold seafood tapas like *berberechos* (cockles), *anchoas* (anchovies), *boquerones* (anchovies in vinegar) or *navajas* (razor shells) tend to prevail over the classic fried foods, but if you feel like ordering *patatas bravas, calamares* or *croquetas,* nobody is going to judge you. Around 2–2.30pm, locals will either go home or to a restaurant, but you can also stay and fill up with more solid tapas. Most traditional *vermuteries* close at around 3.30pm, at which time you'll probably need a good siesta – that's what most *barcelonins* will certainly be doing.

Choosing the right place for fer el vermut

Nowadays, as long as you can order beer and olives, even the simplest bar can be used as a place for *vermut* but, for a more sensual and authentic experience, you're strongly

The Catalan Version of Aperitivo

It is said that the first person to introduce vermouth to Spain was Flaminio Mezzalama, an Italian businessman from Turin who opened two bars in 1902 in Barcelona marketing Martini & Rossi products. These bars – one of them is today the Grill Room in Carrer Escudallers, and the other a jewellery store in Passeig de Gràcia – quickly became the most luxurious bars in town. Like Italians with aperitivo, the concept of having light snacks along with a drink was already present in Catalonia, but it wasn't until the innovative drink named vermouth started gaining popularity that locals began to use the expression *fer el vermut,* literally meaning 'do some vermouth'.

encouraged to look for a bodega (wine cellar) or *vermuteria*, two types of traditional bar targeting locals seeking to enjoy this particular celebration. These bars tend to have in-bulk vermouth on their menus, as well as all the tapas that best fit the occasion. Gràcia is not short of them.

Left Grill Room, one of the first bars in Barcelona to serve *vermut*
Below Bottles of *vermut*

FAR LEFT: GUILLEM LOPEZ/ ALAMY STOCK PHOTO ©
LEFT: CRISTINA ARIAS/GETTY IMAGES ©

25 Sustainable SHOPPING

SHOPPING | ECO-FRIENDLY | RESPONSIBLE TOURISM

The historically left-wing district of Gràcia is today filled with countless organic stores selling all types of eco-friendly products. Fair-trade clothes, jewellery made from recycled materials, vegan cosmetics, in-bulk soap, organic food or even plastic-free nappies (diapers) are just some of the things you can buy here. Gràcia is where you'll find the largest concentration of sustainable shops in all of Spain.

How to

Getting there Fontana Metro station.

Getting around Gràcia is best explored on foot.

Local tip Remember that many local shops close at lunch time, from 2pm to 4pm. Check online for opening hours.

Finding your store Eco-shops are scattered around a big area, so have a list of the shops you want to visit before getting here.

Ethical jewellery A number of outlets specialise in producing jewellery responsibly. For instance, **LUM Ethical Jewellery** fabricates its own lab diamonds and only uses recycled metals and fair-mined gold (gold certified to come from small mines where human rights are respected). Similarly, **Joyería Koetanía** makes jewels with certified conflict-free diamonds. The finished items are always produced locally.

Fair trade and ecological clothes Gràcia is also great for sustainable fashion, a concept that involves buying clothes created with environmentally friendly materials and, if imported, produced in workshops where workers are not being exploited. Additionally some stores, like the family-owned **VELVET BCN**, also work with brands that are heavily involved in social projects in developing countries.

Graneria Sala Shopping in bulk has become a big deal in Gràcia. From lentils to almonds, pasta and Indian spices, buyers come with their own bags or jars and buy just the amount they need, making it an essential part of sustainable shopping. Curious visitors should know, however, that this isn't a new hipster trend; Graneria Sala (Travessera de Gràcia 137) has been doing it since 1885. This traditional shop still keeps its former doors and shutters, and functions as it used to more than 130 years ago, making it a must-see attraction in Gràcia.

Left, bottom left Eco-friendly goods at Olokuti

Best Eco-Friendly Shops in Gràcia

Olokuti Pioneers in sustainable shopping in Barcelona, selling clothes, accessories, food, cosmetics and more. Products for both adults and kids.

Molsa Cooperative supermarket offering organic and ecological products under its own brands.

Gra de Gràcia In-bulk natural products, from cereals to pasta and spices. No plastics used.

Green Lifestyle Ecological fashion, selling clothes with 100% organic natural fabrics and produced by independent designers within Europe.

Amapola Vegan Shop From sandals to scarves, shoes and purses, everything is 100% vegan.

Recommended by Jaume Company, *founder of Olokuti. @olokuti*

26 Fantastical Park GÜELL

ARCHITECTURE | ART | HISTORY

Park Güell is one the most outstanding examples of Catalan modernism, an architectural masterpiece designed by Gaudí where impossible undulating forms covered in colourful broken-tile mosaics make the park's landscape come to life. With one of the best views of Barcelona, no wonder Park Güell has become one of the most renowned tourist attractions in the city.

ALEXANDER PROKOPENKO/SHUTTERSTOCK ©

How to

Getting there There are two metro stations nearby: Lesseps (10 minutes from gate to the monumental area) and Vallcarca (10 minutes from the western park entrance).

When to go To avoid the crowds, go on weekdays at 9.30am, when the park opens.

Monumental area You pay for entering the monumental area, the area designed by Gaudí. The rest of the park is free of charge.

Getting tickets General admission is €10. Tickets can be bought on the official website (https://parkguell.barcelona/en).

JON HICKS/GETTY IMAGES ©

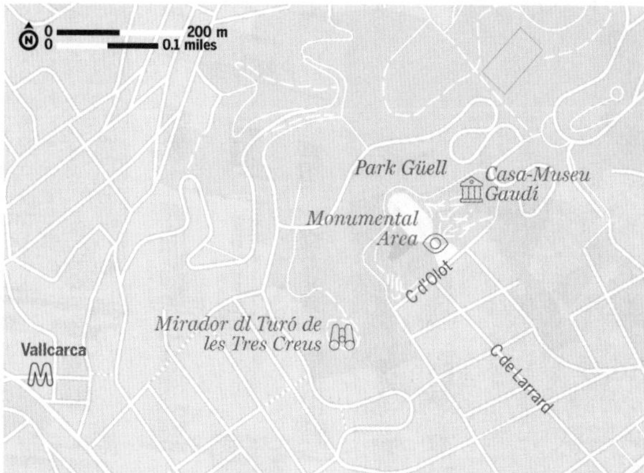

Park Güell wasn't intended to be a park Eusebi Güell wanted Gaudí to build a residential area for wealthy families, far from the chaos of the city. Construction began in 1900, but the project never managed to trigger the necessary interest from the Barcelona elite, so it was abandoned in 1914, becoming a big private garden instead. Güell decided to give it to the Barcelona administration, which opened it to the public in 1926. In a matter of years, it became one of the most visited spots in the city.

Antoni Gaudí lived the last years of his life in the park Out of the 60 houses that were originally planned, only two were built, one of which was acquired by the very same architect in 1906, who lived there with his family until he died in 1926. Today, his former house has become **Casa Museu Gaudí**, a museum aimed at showing Gaudí's most personal and religious side. A separate ticket is required.

Mirador del Turó de les Tres Creus Anything outside of the monumental area is called the forest area, an actual city park where *barcelonins* like to hang out. **Turó de les Tres Creus** is its highest point, a viewpoint from where you can enjoy panoramic city views, and can find a Calvary-shaped monument made by Antoni Gaudí.

Left Dragon Stairway
Bottom left Sala Hipòstila

Monumental Area Highlights

The monumental area was intended to be the common areas of the condominium. All of its elements were built between 1900 and 1914.

Entrance The stately entrance has endless references to industrial development, the Catalan elite and heaven.

Casa del Guarda The building where the caretaker used to live.

Dragon Stairway An elegant staircase featuring the internationally famous colourful salamander.

La Plaça The main square surrounded by the undulating bench, from where you can take in the city's most popular postcard view.

Sala Hipòstila The area marked by the 86 columns that support La Plaça.

Gràcia's Lively SQUARES

LOCAL LIFE | BARS | HISTORY

There is no better way to experience the real, bohemian atmosphere of Gràcia and its local Catalan culture than sitting at the bar terrace of any of its several *plaças* (squares), each one having one little piece of the history of Barcelona to tell.

MARC SOLER/ALAMY STOCK PHOTO ©

How to

Getting there Fontana metro station.

When to go Visit from 7.30pm to 9.30pm, when the squares are packed with locals. Weekends from 12.30pm to 2.30pm is a good time too, when they gather for *vermut*.

Local tip Buying a beer can from the local *supermercado* and sitting in any *plaça* is a common habit among locals. While technically not legal, authorities turn a blind eye.

Gaudí's first house A short walk from Fontana metro, explore Islamic-inspired Casa Vicenç.

KAUKA JARVI/SHUTTERSTOCK ©

Independent Spirit

Gràcia used to be an independent locality Go ramble the alleys of Gràcia and notice how this village-like district feels different from the rest, perhaps because for three different periods throughout the 19th century it was an independent municipality from Barcelona. Its former town council is located in **Plaça de la Vila de Gràcia**, the nerve centre of the district, which features **Campanar de Gràcia**, a 33m clock tower made by Catalan architect Antoni Rovira i Trias – the same person who designed the popular Mercat de Sant Antoni. This structure has become a real symbol for *graciencs*, the bell used to warn of the arrival of Spanish soldiers during the 1870 riots, a protest against army conscription.

The busiest plaça Often said to be the most animated and fun *plaça* in the district, **Plaça**

MARIAJOSE LIU/ALAMY STOCK PHOTO ©

Feel Like Watching a Movie?

Finding a cinema with movies not dubbed into Spanish is not an easy task in this country but in Gràcia, you have **Cines Verdi**, one of the few that shows all movies in the original version. This is also a temple for independent-film lovers: it always has the best range of rarely seen movies.

Top left Plaça del Sol **Left** Plaça del Poble Romaní **Above** Campanar de Gràcia clock tower, Plaça de la Vila de Gràcia

del Sol a meeting point par excellence. Locals know that finding an available table in the square can prove challenging so instead, the ground of Plaça del Sol has become a common spot for people to gather around in circles, drinking something from the nearby liquor shops. It gets so packed that a playground was recently built right in the middle of it, but it didn't make any difference, since some parents join the youth while their kids are being entertained, a pretty common Spanish habit.

Gràcia Arts

Rumba Catalana Just as the Roma people in Andalusia were the biggest contributors to developing flamenco, in Catalonia, they were the inventors of rumba catalana, a musical genre whose rhythms are derived from flamenco. One of the pioneers of this genre was El Pescaílla, a local Roma singer who popularised rumba catalana in the district of Gràcia. Today, **Plaça del Raspall** and **Plaça del Poble Romaní** are home to a Roma

Bomb Shelters in Places de Gràcia

During the Spanish Civil War (1936–39), Barcelona was heavily bombed by anti-Republican forces, a time when *graciencs* joined together to build up to 90 bomb shelters across Gràcia. Their initial idea was to build one main shelter under each *plaça*, connected to each other via tunnels. Over the following decades, most of them were destroyed but today, you can still visit the remains of the shelter located under Plaça del Diamant. Previously arranged guided visits (barcelona.cat/en) are available on Sunday.

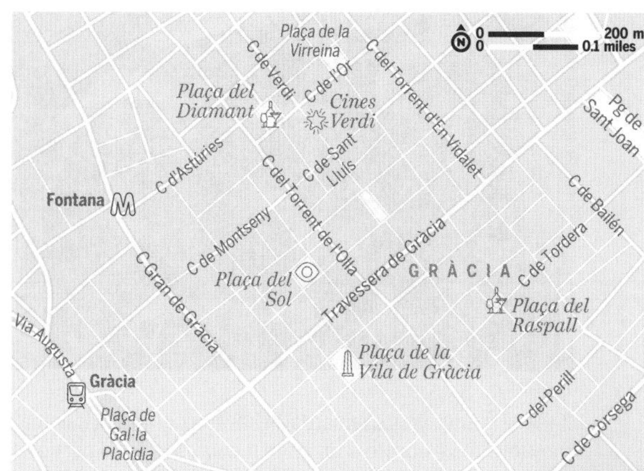

community that has lived in the neighbourhood for more than 300 years, and is undoubtedly part of Gràcia's spirit. The bars at Plaça del Raspall are cheaper than in any other *plaça*.

Colometa Mercè Rodoreda was the most influential contemporary Catalan writer of the twentieth centry. Her bestseller *Plaça del Diamant* tells the story of Colometa, a young Catalan woman who lived during the Spanish Republic and civil war, times in which women were considered second-class citizens. Her story is a recognition of all the Colometas who lived under the will of her husbands. The book takes place in **Plaça del Diamant**, today a socialising point with many bars and a statue of Colometa.

Left *Colometa* statue by Xavier Medina-Campeny, Plaça del Diamant
Below A rumba catalana performance

FAR LEFT: WHOIFNOTME/STOCKIMO/ALAMY STOCK PHOTO ©; LEFT: DAVE G. HOUSER/ALAMY STOCK PHOTO ©

Cultural Immersion at Festa Major de Gràcia

THE OLDEST STREET PARTY IN BARCELONA

One of the biggest street parties in Barcelona takes place during August in the bohemian district of Gràcia, a week-long cultural festival, nationally acclaimed for its Catalan folklore events, creatively decorated streets and night concerts. Whether you are a partygoer or a family with kids, go to Festa Major de Gràcia for a real Catalan cultural immersion.

Left, middle Street decorations during Festa Major de Gràcia **Right** A traditional Catalan *castell* (human castle)

ELEVENSTUDIO/SHUTTERSTOCK ©

If there is anything Spaniards all have in common, it is that they love to celebrate and, when it comes to local parties, all generations do it together. If you happen to order a mojito from a random stall in a *Harry Potter*–themed street surrounded by kids, don't worry: the local people won't judge you, because this is what Festa Major de Gràcia is all about.

During Festa Major de Gràcia, residents from Gràcia test their creative skills by decorating their streets with different themes, ranging from current political topics to cartoons, countries or any exotic location.

Celebrate like the locals do by strolling down these village-like streets while admiring 2m-high action figures made of recycled materials and ordering *canyes* from any of the improvised street-bar counters. *Star Wars*, *Jurassic Park*, Mexican stereotypes or even a funny summary of the Spain–Catalonia conflict, always from a Catalan point of view, are a few examples of the types of decoration you will encounter, all of them competing for the best-decorated-street award.

Meanwhile, the whole district is overrun by the *correfocs* (fire dancers), *castellers* (people forming human castles) and *cap-grossos* (big heads), all part of the diverse and extremely unique Catalan folklore.

At night, *sardanistes* (traditional Catalan dancers) and *havaneres* (the Catalan version of contradance) are replaced by the most relevant Catalan rock stars, who perform in the different scenarios located in the different plazas. The narrow lanes of Gràcia become busier than ever, random drink stalls pop up in every corner and things start getting wild. This is probably not the best time for

IAKOV FILIMONOV/SHUTTERSTOCK ©

FUNKYFROGSTOCK/SHUTTERSTOCK ©

families to roam around, but this epic festival lasts for one entire week, so just come back the next day for an extra dose of local celebration.

Festa Major de Gràcia is more than a popular party, however. It's an event that has taken place for more than 200 years, since a group of monks started celebrating the Assumption of Mary on 15 August 1812, after their monastery was torn down and they were forced to move to the district of Gràcia.

> ...when it comes to local parties, all generations do it together.

At that time, Gràcia was just a small rural settlement but, in 1850, with the district's emancipation from Barcelona and its industrialisation, this celebration began to evolve from a religious-based festival to a civic party where local religious symbols *(enramadas)* were replaced by the secular ornaments used today. Over the following years, Festa Major de Gràcia became a celebration that is now attended by nearly two million people every year.

Best Festes Majors in Barcelona

Festes de Gràcia is one of the most popular *festes majors*, but most districts in Barcelona have their own, typically offering similar events and activities. Catalans call them *festes del barri* (neighbourhood parties) and they are all free, very local, and so much fun. They last for about a week, and here's a list of the best ones with approximate dates:

Festa de Poble Sec Third week of July

Festa de Sants Last week of August

Festa del Poble Nou Mid-September

Festa de la Mercè (all Barcelona) Last week of September

Festa de la Barceloneta End of September–beginning of October

Listings

BEST OF THE REST

Late Night & Music Bars

Heliogàbal €
Best cultural bar for live music since 1995. It is known for promoting Catalan artists like Manel or Mishima. It also organises book launches and photography exhibitions.

Elephanta €€
With over 40 brands of gin, this modern and elegant bar was popular for its gin and tonics, even before the drink became a national trend.

L'Entresòl €
Musical bar with a resident DJ mainly playing indie and rock.

Soda Acústic €
This cosy bar organises frequent jazz and blues concerts, normally played by local artists. Drinks are pretty affordable.

Japanese Small Eats

Kibuka €€
The most popular sushi place in the neighbourhood. Not the best sushi you'll taste, but at this price, there's nothing better. There are two restaurants, both in Gràcia. Expect a long wait for lunch on weekdays as people line up for the affordable *menú del día*.

Kakigori €
A cute take-away shop specialising in *kakigori* (Japanese ice cream), but also *dorayaki* (red-bean pancake) and *onigiri* (rice balls).

Vegan & Vegetarian Meals

Quinoa Bar €
Bowls, burgers, wraps, cakes and all types of healthy, vegan food. The carrot cake with coconut milk is superb. Wine and beers are also available.

Dolce Pizza y Los Veganos €
Pizzas made with vegan cheese, but also a wide variety of meet-free pasta. It also has vegan hot dogs and burgers, as well as a few vegetarian options.

Veg World India €€
Indian restaurant with a beautiful set-up, serving several vegetarian tandooris, curries, and naans. Try the bread with mango.

Traditional Menus

Yesterday €
Market cuisine selling one of the best value-for-money *menús del día* (daily set menus) in the district. It mostly offers home-made Spanish food, but also occasional international dishes.

La Pubilla €€
Traditional Catalan food with a touch of modernity, always cooked with the freshest ingredients from nearby Mercat de la Llibertat. While pricier than others, the *menú del día* is delicious, but you must book in advance.

Bar of Mercat de la Llibertat €
Located inside Mercat de la Llibertat, this extremely local bar is popular for breakfast, when you can order a dish of *saltxitxes amb tomàquet* (Catalan sausages with tomato sauce). Ordering a *canya* in the morning is fine too.

Cal Boter €
A traditional restaurant serving classics like *trinxat de la Cerdanya* (cabbage with black sausage), *bacallà a la llauna* (local cod-fish recipe) and other Catalan specialities. Super affordable *menú del día* but do go early (around 1.30pm) to avoid long queues.

Pollería Fontana €

One of those local restaurants where you can try rare finds such as *mandonguilles amb sèpia* (beef meatballs with cuttlefish), a strange combination typically eaten in those Catalan regions squeezed between the Mediterranean and the Pyrenees.

International Quick Bites

Petra €

This tiny Lebanese restaurant is famous for serving the best *shawarma* in Gràcia. The crunchy falafels are pretty amazing too. Other Lebanese delicacies like hummus, *arayes* (meat-stuffed pitas) and *kofta* (meat skewers) are also available.

La Empanadería de Gracia €

Take-away restaurant with dozens of Argentinian empanadas to choose from, some of them with pretty creative fillings, like wild boar or goats' cheese with pear and almonds.

Wok Verdi €

The classic East Asian street-food eatery, but an institution for being one of the very first of its kind.

Eco-Friendly Shops

Olokuti

The pioneer of sustainable shopping in Gràcia, selling all types of items, from organic cotton T-shirts to bags made with recycled materials, and baby items made with LIVA silicon. A reference point in eco-shopping.

VELVET BCN Moda Sostenible y Comercio Justo

A fashion shop specialising in fair-trade clothes and those made with organic cotton, ecological dyes and recycled plastics.

Espai Amaru

An exquisite pottery workshop, but also a store where useful ceramic items, such as bowls or plates, are sold. The products are exclusively made of water, mud and natural glaze.

KAUKA JARVI / SHUTTERSTOCK ©

Plaça del Nord

LUM Ethical Jewellery

An eco-jewellery maker that fabricates pieces on demand, ranging from €200 to €5000. The diamonds used are lab created and the gold is certified fair-mined.

Plaças to Linger

Plaça de la Virreina

A pedestrian square with a beautiful, 19th-century church named **Església de Sant Joan**. Some claim its underground chapel was created by Gaudí.

Plaça del Nord

This is the most local of all the area's squares, as it is relatively distant from the leisure areas. Try the local, homemade tapas from **El Far del Nord**.

Plaça de Rovira i Trias

Named after the architect who designed it, who was also Gaudí's disciple. It houses the most famous craft beer bar in the neighbourhood, La Rovira.

CAMP NOU,
PEDRALBES &
LA ZONA ALTA
ARCHITECTURE | LOCAL FOOD | NATURE

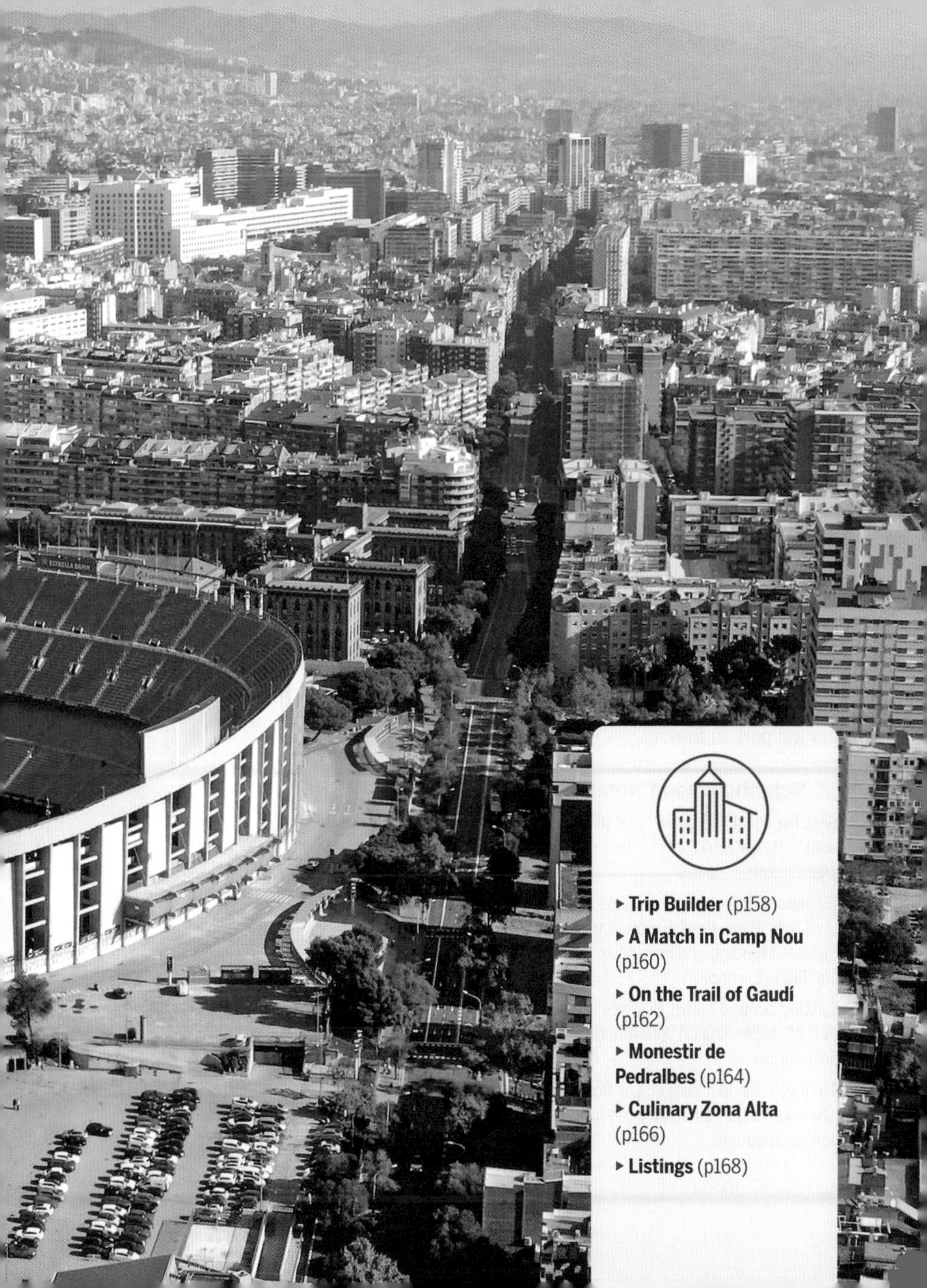

CAMP NOU, PEDRALBES & LA ZONA ALTA Trip Builder

TAKE YOUR PICK OF MUST-SEES AND HIDDEN GEMS

The upper-class neighbourhood of Zona Alta is a must-see for those interested in the fine-dining scene, but also for its rarely visited architectural delights. The district is also home to the FC Barcelona stadium, and nature lovers will enjoy hiking in Collserola, the only natural park in the city.

Neighbourhood Notes

Best for Local fine dining, nightlife, nature, Barça World, off-the-beaten-path architecture.

Transport Useful metro stations include Les Corts, Palau Reial, Gràcia, Sant Gervasi, Muntaner, La Bonanova, Sarrià and Reina Elisenda.

Getting around Metro, bus, taxi or by foot, depending on your itinerary/ destination.

Tip If you are on a budget, Les Corts is where you'll find the most economical accommodation.

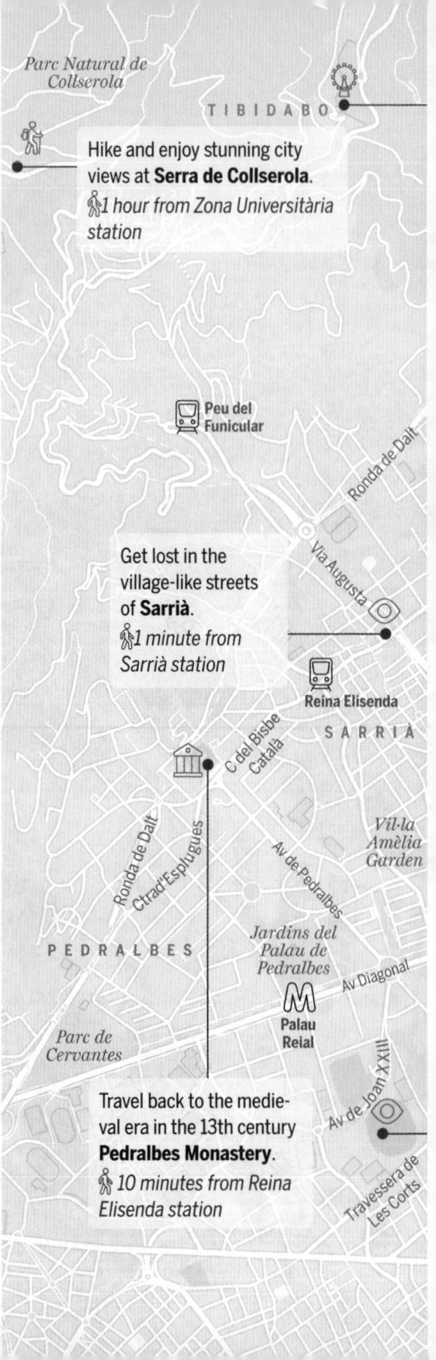

Spend some time in one of the oldest amusement parks in Europe at **Tibidabo**.

The funicular is 1.2km (20 minutes) from Avinguda Tibidabo metro station

Visit Gaudí-designed **Torre Bellesguard**, a former medieval castle restored into a beautiful modernist building.

10 minutes from Avinguda Tibidabo station

Look for the best *tortilla de patatas* (egg and potato omelette) in the city at **Mantequerías Pirenaicas**.

5 minutes from Muntaner station

C de Muntaner

Av Diagonal

Diagonal

C de Balmes

Parc del Turó

Plaça de Francesc Macià

C del Comte d'Urgell

L'EIXAMPLE

Av de Josep Tarradellas

Savour the local **fine-dining scene** in Sant Gervasi in a restaurant like Barra Alta.

3 minutes from Gràcia station

Witness the magic offered by some of the world's best football players at **FC Barcelona stadium**.

5 minutes from Les Corts station

N 0 1 km
0 0.5 miles

28 A Match in CAMP NOU

SPORT | LEISURE | LOCAL

Imagine enjoying the feats of some of football's greatest players, surrounded by up to 100,000 raucous fans. Barça is considered one of the best teams in the world, and attending one of their matches in Camp Nou is more than just watching a football game: it's an unrivalled experience.

CHRISTIAN BERTRAND/SHUTTERSTOCK ©

How to

Getting there There are four metro stations close to the stadium: Collblanc and Badal and Les Corts and Maria Cristina.

When to go The football season runs from mid-August to mid-June. For exact dates and times, check the official website.

Getting tickets Head to the official website (fcbarcelona.com/en) for tickets.

Costs Prices range from €10 to €1000, depending on the opponent, competition and seat.

YURI TURKOV/SHUTTERSTOCK ©

The largest stadium in Europe With a capacity of nearly 100,000 people, Camp Nou is the largest football stadium on the European continent and the fifth largest in the world. It translates as 'New Field', so called because it replaced the former stadium named Camp de les Corts back in 1957.

Més que un Club Meaning 'more than a club', FC Barcelona's motto expresses its willingness to go beyond being just a football club. It is the most important sports institution in Catalonia and an ambassador and promoter of the Catalan culture. Many Catalans see Barça as a symbol of their national identity.

Visiting the stadium and museum Those who miss the chance to attend a Barça game have the great alternative of visiting the Barça Museum and the stadium premises. The museum features all the trophies and titles achieved by the team, as well as a comprehensive, visual exploration of its 120-year history. The tour around the stadium can include visiting the press room, walking along the pitch or even checking out the changing rooms, depending on the tickets you buy.

Left Match day at Camp Nou
Below left FC Barcelona tunnel, which leads players to the field

Make the Most of a Barça game

Don't get the cheapest seat Camp Nou is very large and the cheapest seats may have restricted visibility. Try to aim for a low-midrange location, like the first or second corner stands.

Experience the local football vibe Before the match, several bars around the stadium are filled with locals gathering for celebration.

Plan your arrival and leaving time To avoid missing any action, aim to get to the stadium an hour before game time. Leave 30 minutes afterwards, to avoid the human avalanche heading to the metro station.

Marcel Tomàs, *member of FC Barcelona*

29 On the Trail of GAUDÍ

ARCHITECTURE | ART | CULTURE

Before creating the undulating shapes and tree-like columns that define his naturalist style, Antoni Gaudí went through orientalist and neo-Gothic periods. Zona Alta is home to some of his most important – and least well-known – works from that era, easily visited on a self-guided walking tour.

MIGUEL SOTOMAYOR/GETTY IMAGES ©

How to

Getting there Catch the metro to Avinguda Tibidado, 1km on foot from Torre Bellesguard.

Getting around On foot. The total itinerary length is about 4km.

Entry tickets Torre Bellesguard (via official website; portalgaudi.cat); Font d'Hércules (free of charge); Colegio de las Teresianas (only possible to view from outside); Pabellons Güell (expected to reopen in 2022 after restoration work).

Tip Start your tour at Torre Bellesguard, so you go downhill all the way.

The Earlier Years of Antoni Gaudí

During the last two decades of the 19th century, most Gaudí works were inspired by Islamic-Hispanic art and then Medieval Gothic, rather than natural elements. Some fine examples from that era are:

Casa Vicenç (pictured above; Gràcia, Barcelona)

Palau Güell (La Rambla, Barcelona)

Bodegues Güell (Sitges)

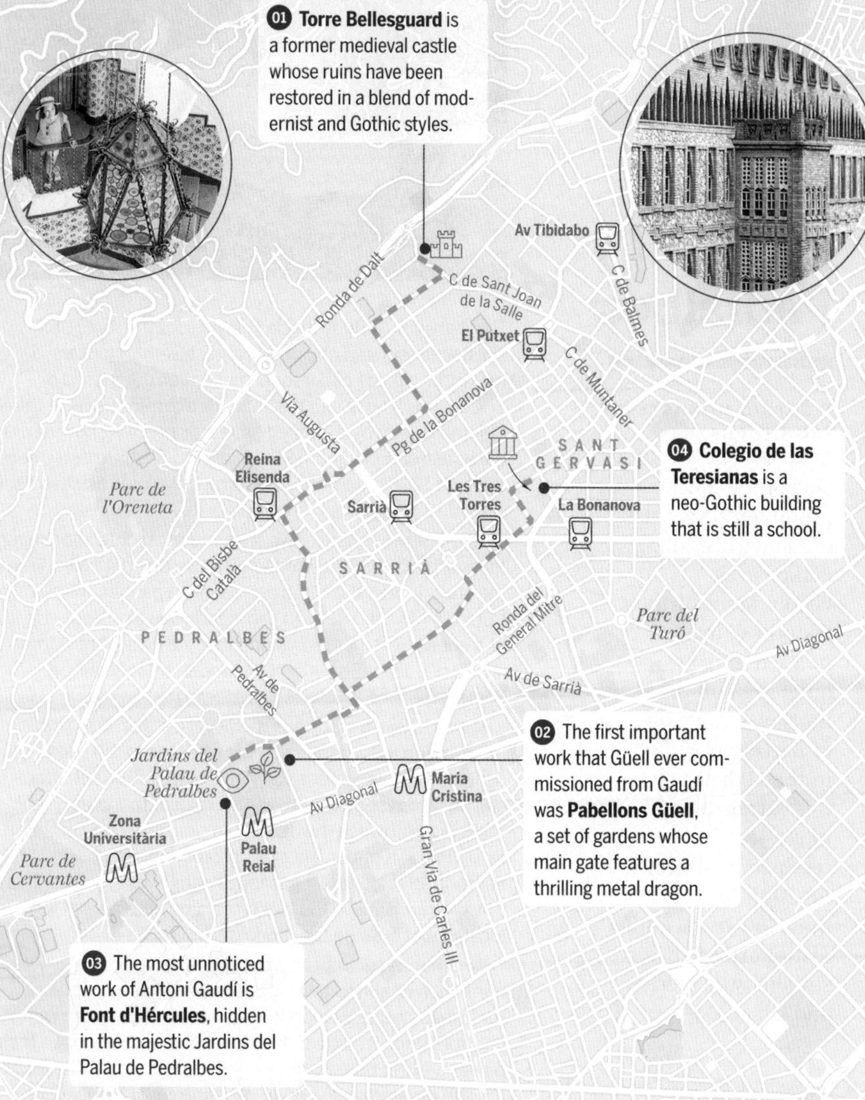
0 1 km
0 0.5 miles
01 Torre Bellesguard is a former medieval castle whose ruins have been restored in a blend of modernist and Gothic styles.
Av Tibidabo
Ronda de Dalt
C de Sant Joan de la Salle
C de Balmes
El Putxet
C de Muntaner
Via Augusta
Pg de la Bonanova
SANT GERVASI
04 Colegio de las Teresianas is a neo-Gothic building that is still a school.
Reina Elisenda
Parc de l'Oreneta
Sarrià
Les Tres Torres
La Bonanova
SARRIÀ
C del Bisbe Català
Ronda del General Mitre
Parc del Turó
Av Diagonal
PEDRALBES
Av de Pedralbes
Av de Sarrià
02 The first important work that Güell ever commissioned from Gaudí was Pabellons Güell, a set of gardens whose main gate features a thrilling metal dragon.
Jardins del Palau de Pedralbes
Maria Cristina
Av Diagonal
Zona Universitària
Palau Reial
Parc de Cervantes
Gran Via de Carles III
03 The most unnoticed work of Antoni Gaudí is Font d'Hércules, hidden in the majestic Jardins del Palau de Pedralbes.

Monestir de Pedralbes

PHILIPPE LISSAC/GETTY IMAGES ©

A GOTHIC MONASTERY FROM THE 14TH CENTURY

One of the most prominent examples of Catalan Gothic is the barely visited Monestir de Pedralbes, located in a seductively quiet area on the northwestern edge of Barcelona. Built in the 14th century, this extraordinary monastery has retained its original function for more than 700 years, and is distinguished by its simplicity, austerity and silence.

Left Marble tomb of Queen Elisenda
Middle The monastery's courtyard
Right Religious tilework

The highlight of Monestir de Pedralbes is the three-storey cloister considered one of the largest Gothic cloisters in the world, a place of personal meditation composed of 26 columns whose capitals represent the emblems of the Montcada and royal family. Not less impressive, however, is the actual church, another outstanding Gothic masterpiece that was built in only one year, an unbelievable achievement according to experts.

Right between these two sites is a sepulchre containing the marble tomb of a woman with two distinct faces. From the church side, the tomb represents a penitent nun, while from the cloister side you can clearly see the silhouette of a queen, with her crown and fancy jewels. That woman is in fact Queen Elisenda, the founder of Monestir de Pedralbes.

It was 1326, the glorious medieval Catalan era. With King Jaume II in poor health, his wife Queen Elisenda decided to build a monastery as a place of retreat after she became widowed. It wasn't a regular monastery, but the queen provided it with certain privileges, one of them being to put it under the city's protection, which was committed to defend it in case of danger or invasion. This privilege is visible in the two remaining defensive towers located just outside the monastery.

Another peculiarity was that, throughout its history, the nuns that inhabited the monastery were all daughters of renowned nobles and aristocrats, powerful women who controlled the wealth of the monastery and exercised their power beyond being simple nuns in the cloister. These women created and shaped the essence of Monestir de Pedralbes.

SELENARUS/GETTY IMAGES ©

JOAN_BAUTISTA/SHUTTERSTOCK ©

Monestir de Pedralbes today

From its foundation in 1327 until 1983, Monestir de Pedralbes was always inhabited by nuns who carried out a monastic life. Today, the remaining nuns live in houses adjacent to the monastery, but it has never lost its worship function. The church is fully functional and the nuns celebrate a daily service at 7pm (noon on Sundays).

That monastic life is today represented in the monastery's different rooms, which are all open to visitors. The kitchen, stables and even the refectory will give you an idea of what convent life used to be like until not many years ago. The former dormitories house some of the monastery's treasures, including pieces of art and manuscripts.

...remaining nuns live in houses adjacent to the monastery, but it has never lost its worship function.

Monestir de Pedralbes is an attraction not to be missed, but also one of Barcelona's best-kept secrets, both among locals and foreigners.

Prehistoric Sacred Site

Visitors can't stop wondering about the unpolished rock that nearly blocks the way into one of the main gates of the monastery. It isn't just a random stone taken from the nearby hills of Collserola, but a prehistoric relic, a buried menhir, and the only known megalithic monument in the city of Barcelona. Historians believe that Queen Elisenda and King James II chose the site because it had been considered sacred for several generations.

The Catalan Gothic

The 14th and 15th centuries were the most splendid era in the history of Catalonia, a period where Catalans benefited hugely from maritime trade. Enormous wealth was created in the city, with different guilds used to create buildings that helped develop the Catalan Gothic architectural style (similar to the European Gothic but unique in its austerity and simplicity). Today, you can find innumerable examples of Catalan Gothic in Barcelona, the finest being the Basilica de Santa Maria del Mar, built with the wealth of merchants and ship owners; La Llotja, a medieval commercial market; and Palau Berenguer d'Aguilar, a former palace housing the Museu Picasso.

By Robin Townsend, *photojournalist and historian, @robin_townsend*

30 Culinary ZONA ALTA

FOOD | LOCAL | CULTURE

Zona Alta is a surprisingly local area of Barcelona. When it comes to restaurants, here you won't find the tourist traps that abound in other neighbourhoods. As the wealthiest district in Barcelona, Zona Alta is filled with some of the most exquisite restaurants in town, from Michelin-starred delights to elegant tapas joints, and also a few local eateries worth a try.

XAVIER LORENZO/LONELY PLANET ©

How to

Getting here Most restaurants are close to Muntaner and Sant Gervasi stations.

Average cost Restaurants cater to all wallets, with meals from €5 to €350 per person.

Local tip Keep in mind that local kitchens in Barcelona (and throughout Spain) don't serve food all day long. Typically, lunchtime runs from 1.30pm to 3.30pm, and dinner from 9pm to 11pm.

Reserve your table For the best restaurants, it is recommended to book in advance.

EUROPA PRESS NEWS/GETTY IMAGES ©

The art of the Spanish tapa Tapas are not just the Spanish staple, but a way of life. They are often related to happiness, made to share and are typically accompanied by a glass of wine or *caña.* From the Atlantic coast to the Mediterranean provinces and the arid plains around Madrid, Spanish cuisine is extremely diverse but, if there is one thing that unites all Spaniards, it is their tapas lifestyle. In Zona Alta, however, young, ambitious chefs have put faith in taking this lifestyle to the next level by opening tapas restaurants that also offer an innovative culinary experience.

Hunting the best tortilla de patatas in Barcelona Cooking and achieving the right texture for a *tortilla de patatas* (egg and potato omelette) is not an easy task. It's an art and, unlike in Madrid, tasting a decent *tortilla de patatas* can prove challenging. This isn't an issue in Zona Alta, however: it's home to the largest concentration of local eateries serving mouthwatering tortillas. Favourites include Mantequerías Pireneicas, Les Truites and El Rebost del Galvany.

Michelin-star restaurants Four out of the 22 Michelin-star restaurants in Barcelona are located in Zona Alta, including one of the only two with three stars. All of them serve different types of Catalan and Spanish high cuisine. The starred restaurants are Àbac, Hisop, Hofmann and Via Veneto.

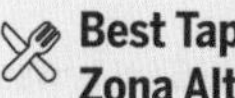
Left *Jamón* (ham) **Bottom left** Chef Jordi Cruz of Àbac restaurant

Best Tapas in Zona Alta

Tapas are ideal for any budget. The final bill may run from €20 to €150 per person depending on what you order.

Bambarol Classic but elaborate Spanish tapas with a large list of chef's specials.

Vivanda Catalan/Mediterranean tapas with a wide variety of fish and meat.

Bisavis Traditional tapas bar that uses the best quality ingredients; has a large selection of wines.

Blavis Creative tapas with Italian and Japanese influences.

Barra alta Large selection of classic, but modern Spanish tapas.

Recommended by Ferran Maicas, *chef and owner of Bambarol*

Listings

BEST OF THE REST

Michelin-star Restaurants

Hisop €€€
The most affordable Michelin-star restaurant in town. It serves innovative, modern Catalan cuisine and changes the menu at the beginning of each season.

Via Veneto €€€
Open since 1967, this was one of the first luxury restaurants to open in the city. The menu features old, traditional Catalan dishes such as *canelons* (cylindrical pasta filled with bechamel and meat, and covered with grilled cheese), but with a Michelin-star twist.

Àbac €€€
If your wallet allows, this three-star gem offers sophisticated dishes from different regions in Spain.

Midrange Restaurants

Coure €€
Modern Catalan cuisine. Don't miss the *croqueta de rabo de toro* (oxtail croquette). Consider ordering the tasting menu.

Bambarol €€
Feast on classic Mediterranean tapas made with the freshest ingredients. Unlike at other tapas joints, the menu is short and simple, assuring the best quality. Great for lunch or dinner, every day of the week.

Bar Omar €€
The menu has a large selection of classic Spanish tapas, but also elaborate dishes like steak tartare in coffee butter or grilled octopus with potato parmentier.

Flash Flash €€
This restaurant still has the pop-art design that it had in the '60s. Its menu features nearly 50 different kinds of *tortilla de patas* as well as complex, exquisite dishes like duck rice with truffle.

Budget Local Eateries

Bodega Josefa €
Whether you come for breakfast, lunch or evening tapas, this old, authentic Spanish bar is worth visiting at any time of the day.

Mantequerías Pirenaicas €
In business for more than 60 years, this small cafe is always packed with locals eating the renowned *tortilla de patatas*. Try the truffle tortilla washed down with the house red.

El Tomàs de Sarrià €
Pretty much any *barceloní* knows about the *patatas bravas* of Can Tomàs, which were once featured in the *Wall Street Journal*.

El Rebost del Galvany €
For a local experience, eat breakfast at this small eatery located inside the architecturally noted Mercat de Galvany.

Budy Café €
A Spanish restaurant serving a wide choice of Mediterranean dishes. The *menú del día* (daily set menu) is one of the best and most affordable in the area.

International Restaurants

La Balmesina €
This small Italian restaurant heads all the best-pizza-in-Barcelona lists. On weekdays for lunch, it offers an excellent daily menu with a large variety of choices.

Hitsumabushi €€
This Japanese-owned restaurant is one of the

most authentic in town. The stewed eel is excellent.

Byblos €

The owner of this restaurant is a charismatic Lebanese who can brag about having the shawarma joint with the longest ordering line in the city.

Gardens & Parks

Jardins del Palau de Pedralbes

The majestic gardens of the former Spanish Royal Spanish Family residence from 1919 to 1931 feature a Gaudí-designed fountain and a fantastic collection of cedars. Hosts the Festival de Pedralbes, a renowned music festival, each summer.

Turó Park

Located next to the bustling Francesc Macià, this quiet park is where locals come to walk around the holm oak forest or read a book under the magnolia trees. Don't miss the statue of Pau Casals, a Catalan musician and one of the world's greatest cellists.

Jardins de la Tamarita

A set of gardens built by the Catalan bourgeoisie in the 19th century around their mansions. Given their former private character, the gardens are filled with ornamental elements, like water fountains, terracotta figures and fancy flowerpots.

Cocktail & Wine Bars

Gimlet €€

A classic, international cocktail bar with a modern atmosphere, this is one of the reference points in Barcelona. The Catalan *cava* mixed with Italian liquors is superb.

Matos Bar de Vins Enoteca €€

This rare find in Sant Gervasi has a vast selection of wines, many of them with tantalisingly obscure designations of origin.

JOAN_BAUTISTA/SHUTTERSTOCK ©

Jardins de la Tamarita

Gourmet Patisseries

Foix de Sarrià €

Up and running since 1886, this patisserie has always combined tradition with innovation, selling all types of cakes, pies and sweets; the lemon pie is unrivalled. There are two branches not far from each other.

Chis & Keik €

Two Catalan guys who lived in Massachusetts for a long time recently opened a patisserie where they create more than 100 types of cheesecake.

La Petita de la Gran €

Classic Spanish pastries, but also cakes and pies with groundbreaking formulas. The pastry chef from this charming patisserie was trained at Hofmann, one of the most renowned hospitality schools.

MONTJUÏC, POBLE SEC & SANT ANTONI

LOCAL CULTURE | URBAN NATURE | CREATIVE EATERIES

MONTJUÏC, POBLE SEC & SANT ANTONI
Trip Builder

TAKE YOUR PICK OF MUST-SEES AND HIDDEN GEMS

With the exception of some top attractions on Montjuïc, this neighbourhood is often overlooked. However, there are many hidden gems, including some of Barcelona's most creative eateries, an open-air book market and an air-raid shelter where you can learn about the city's experiences during the Spanish Civil War.

Neighbourhood Notes

Best for Learning about local life and history.

Transport Well connected by metro; funicular or a cable car from La Barceloneta are also options to Montjuïc.

Getting around Wear comfortable shoes to explore the area on foot.

Tip Plan your visit well, as some places are only accessible on Sundays.

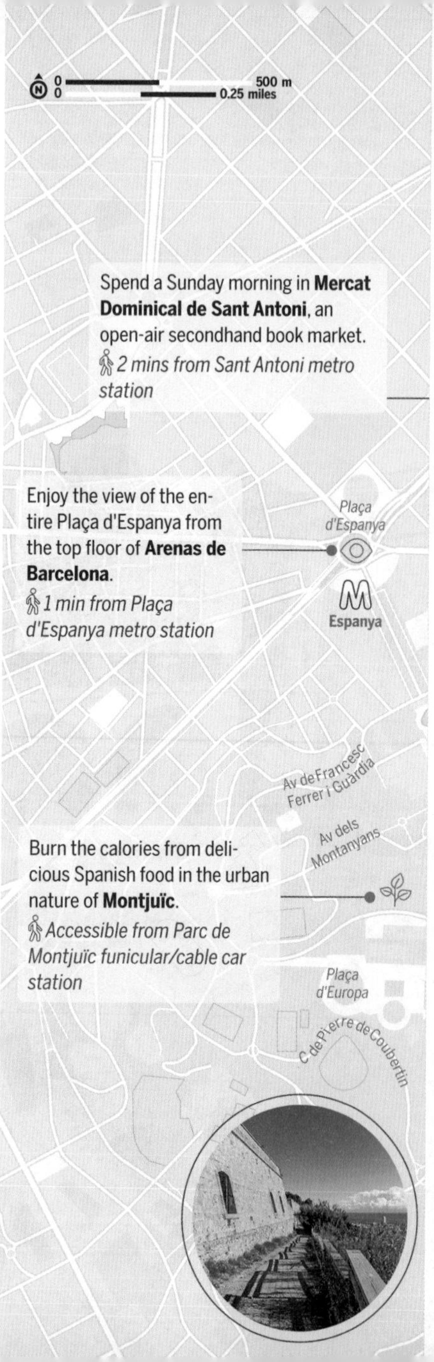
0 500 m
0 0.25 miles
Spend a Sunday morning in Mercat Dominical de Sant Antoni, an open-air secondhand book market.
2 mins from Sant Antoni metro station
Enjoy the view of the entire Plaça d'Espanya from the top floor of Arenas de Barcelona.
1 min from Plaça d'Espanya metro station
Plaça d'Espanya
Espanya
Av de Francesc Ferrer i Guàrdia
Av dels Montanyans
Burn the calories from delicious Spanish food in the urban nature of Montjuïc.
Accessible from Parc de Montjuïc funicular/cable car station
Plaça d'Europa
C de Pierre de Coubertin

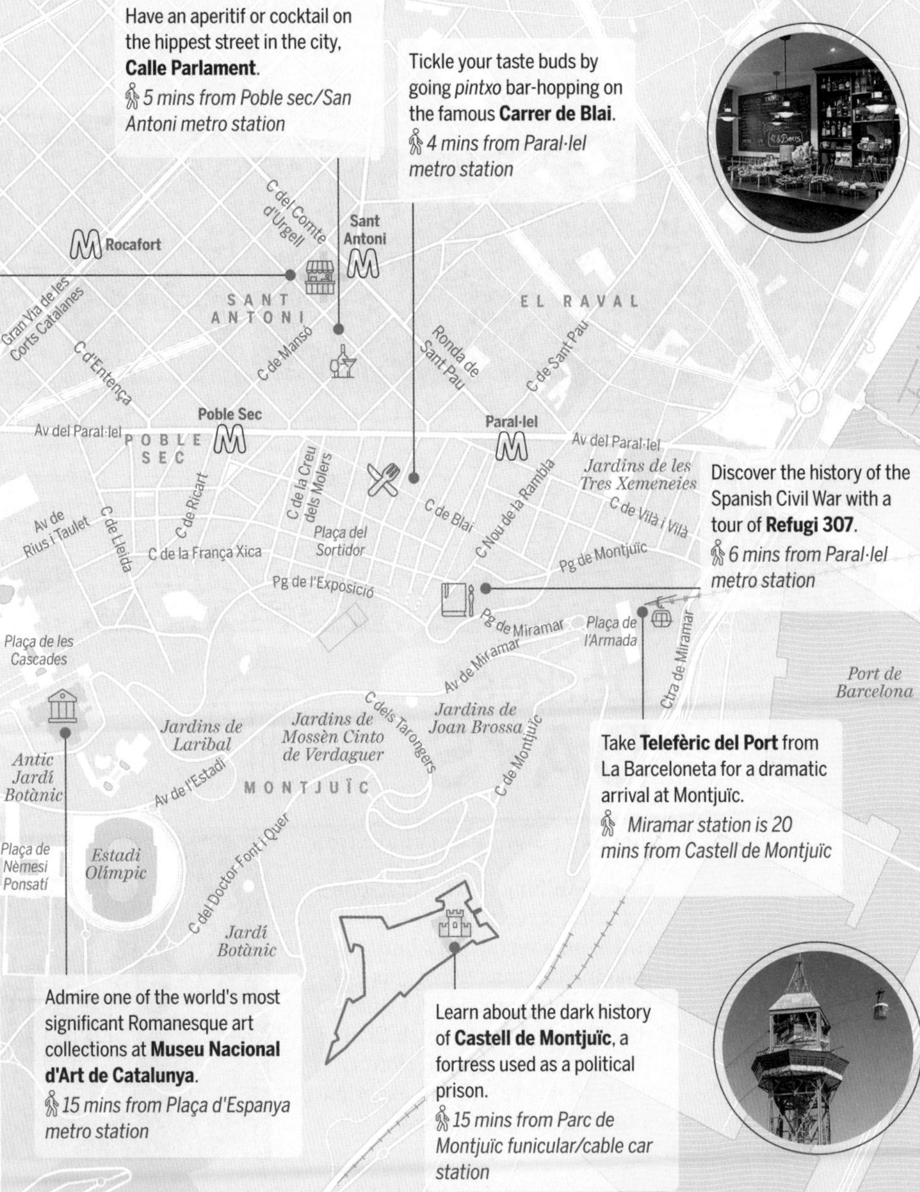

Have an aperitif or cocktail on the hippest street in the city, **Calle Parlament**.
5 mins from Poble sec/San Antoni metro station
Tickle your taste buds by going *pintxo* bar-hopping on the famous **Carrer de Blai**.
4 mins from Paral·lel metro station
Rocafort
Sant Antoni
C del Comte d'Urgell
Gran Via de les Corts Catalanes
SANT ANTONI
EL RAVAL
C de Mansó
C d'Entença
Ronda de Sant Pau
C de Sant Pau
Poble Sec
Paral·lel
Av del Paral·lel
POBLE SEC
Av del Paral·lel
Jardins de les Tres Xemeneies
Discover the history of the Spanish Civil War with a tour of **Refugi 307**.
6 mins from Paral·lel metro station
C de la Creu dels Molers
C de Ricart
C de Blai
C Nou de la Rambla
C de Vilà i Vilà
Av de Rius i Taulet
C de Lleida
C de la França Xica
Plaça del Sortidor
Pg de Montjuïc
Pg de l'Exposició
Pg de Miramar
Plaça de l'Armada
Ctra de Miramar
Plaça de les Cascades
Av de Miramar
Port de Barcelona
C dels Tarongers
Jardins de Joan Brossa
Jardins de Laribal
Jardins de Mossèn Cinto de Verdaguer
Antic Jardí Botànic
Av de l'Estadi
MONTJUÏC
C de Montjuïc
Take **Telefèric del Port** from La Barceloneta for a dramatic arrival at Montjuïc.
Miramar station is 20 mins from Castell de Montjuïc
Plaça de Nèmesi Ponsatí
Estadi Olímpic
C del Doctor Font i Quer
Jardí Botànic
Admire one of the world's most significant Romanesque art collections at **Museu Nacional d'Art de Catalunya**.
15 mins from Plaça d'Espanya metro station
Learn about the dark history of **Castell de Montjuïc**, a fortress used as a political prison.
15 mins from Parc de Montjuïc funicular/cable car station

31 Darkest DAYS

HISTORY | CIVIL WAR | EDUCATION

Walking down Barcelona's beautiful streets or sipping a coffee on a terrace, it's hard to imagine the time when this city was heavily bombed and suffered the effects of the Spanish Civil War and its aftermath. Here's a guide to where you can experience a little bit of this history.

VADIM FEDOTOV/SHUTTERSTOCK©

How to

Getting here and around Most of the sights are easily accessible by metro or funicular. The most comfortable way to get to Castell de Montjuïc is to take Telefèric de Montjuïc from the upper funicular station, which saves a 20-minute walk up the hill.

When to go Refugi 307 is only accessible on Sundays by free guided tour. Prior reservation is required via the website (ajuntament.barcelona.cat/museuhistoria/en).

Tip Wear comfortable shoes.

MUHBA (MUSEO DE HISTORIA DE BARCELONA) ©

A City Systematically Bombed

During the Spanish Civil War (1936–39), in which the Nationalist rebels led by General Franco overthrew the Republican government, Barcelona was systematically bombed by the fascist states supporting the Nationalists. During the three years of the war, nearly 194 bombs were dropped on the city, killing 1816 people and injuring 2710, according to one local newspaper. The neighbourhood of Poble Sec was said to be one of the areas in the city most affected by the bombing, due to its proximity to strategic and military targets such as **Castell de Montjuïc**, the **Port of Barcelona** and the power station.

Inside the shelter To protect the neighbourhood's citizens from a series of attacks, **Refugi 307** was built at the foot of Montjuïc.

DFLC PRINTS/SHUTTERSTOCK©

War Stories

A great resource for imagining wartime in Barcelona is the website titled **The city of shelters** (https://ajuntament.barcelona.cat/arqueologiabarcelona/refugis/en), which maps over 1300 shelters and areas affected by air strikes. You can also read the testimonies of those who lived through that time.

Top left Castell de Montjuïc's courtyard
Left Prison door, Castell de Montjuïc
Above Refugio 307

This shelter is one of the best-preserved and most easily accessible among those built in Barcelona during the war. Following an introduction, the guided tour will take you into the shelter, which has a tunnel that's 400m long, 2.10m high, and 1.5–2m wide. As you walk through the dim and narrow path, imagine what it must have been like when up to 2000 residents gathered here to protect themselves from the threat of bombs falling from the sky.

The prisoner's cry After visiting the shelter, you will see some of the area's classic sights from a different perspective – for example, **Castell de Montjuïc**, known for its stunning views of the Mediterranean. The castle was used as a military prison until 1960, incarcerating fascists during the war and Republicans during Franco's dictatorship. In 2018, more than 650 pieces of graffiti inscribed on the walls by prisoners were discovered in the dungeons. Some of them express a sense

Hero of Poble Sec

Francesc Boix, a Catalan photographer and veteran of the Republican army, is a hero of Poble Sec. After his exile in France at the end of the civil war, he was imprisoned in the Nazi Mauthausen concentration camp in Austria, where he worked as a slave in the SS photo lab. He secretly stole the negatives that would later become crucial evidence at the Nuremberg Trials. During Franco's dictatorship, Boix' remarkable story was silenced, but in 2001 a plaque was placed at his **birthplace**, Carrer de Margarit 17. The local **library**, 40m away, is named after him. It has a collection of books on the war and the Holocaust.

Recommended by Nick Lloyd, *author of* Forgotten Places: Barcelona and the Spanish Civil War, *and virtual and in-person tour guide @Civil_War_Spain*

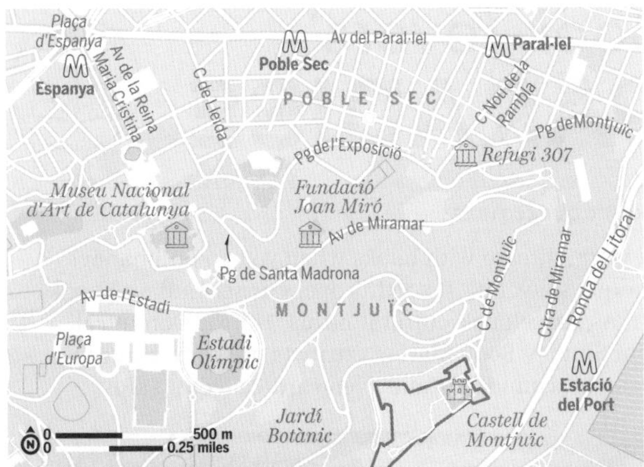

of despair: 'Get me out of here, I'm going crazy'. There are also several hand-drawn calendars, erotic drawings, and daily prison schedules that tell the story of the prisoners' everyday lives. The dungeon section can only be entered during the daily guided tours.

Artists and the war Many artists also found it impossible to ignore this tragedy. Their works, which vividly reflect the mood of the period, can be seen in the famous museums in Montjuïc. **Fundació Joan Miró** has some works related to this theme, such as Man and Woman in Front of a Pile of Excrement, painted in 1935 by Miró, who sensed the growing tension before the war. Also, the **Museu Nacional d'Art de Catalunya** expanded the number of rooms of the permanent collection of works produced during the war in 2021. A total of 108 pieces are on display, including paintings, sculptures and propaganda posters. There's also a section featuring women who played their part in that period, including a portrait of the Republican heroine Lina Ódena, by J Pons, a tribute created after her untimely death in the first months of the war.

Left Photo of Francesc Boix, displayed at a memorial service in Paris **Below** Castell de Montjuïc

32 Book-lovers' PARADISE

UNIQUE SOUVENIRS | BOOKS | COLLECTIBLES

Do you always pack your suitcase with books when you go on holiday? Or are you looking for a unique souvenir? If so, this open-air secondhand book market is the place for you. As Barcelona's cultural nexus, Mercat Dominical de Sant Antoni (Sant Antoni Sunday Book Market) attracts book lovers, geeks hunting for vintage video games, comic fans and even card-collecting kids.

NITO/SHUTTERSTOCK ©

How to

Getting here The closest metro station is Sant Antoni.

When to go Every Sunday from 8.30am to 2pm, year-round. The space is covered, so it's accessible rain or shine.

Top tips If you've bought more than you can fit in your suitcase, ask the seller for an international shipping service. After shopping, enjoy the local custom of *fer el vermut* (take an aperitif) before a late lunch at Calle Parlament, where there are many bars.

KYOKO KAWAGUCHI/LONELY PLANET ©

Far left, bottom left Browsing Mercat Dominical de Sant Antoni book market **Left** Market-goers on La Diada de Sant Jordi (St George's Day)

Eighty-five years of history The market dates to 1937, when it exclusively sold books and collectible items in the current location. Although 80% of the stalls specialise in paper-related products – books, magazines, comics, trading cards, vintage posters – some sell culture-related products such as vinyl, video games and collectible figures.

Treasure hunting With 74 stalls spread across 1800 sq metres around Mercat de Sant Antoni, the market offers anything that could scratch your cultural itch. Language learner? Look for a random local language book that intrigues you at a low cost. Even if you don't understand Spanish or Catalan, it's fun to look for comics or manga titles in those languages. Or you might run into your favourite childhood Nintendo cartridge. Some stalls sell English books too.

Kids' spontaneous social place Circulating around the stalls, you will spot kids exchanging cromos, trading cards of superheroes, sports players and anime characters. Even though it's not an official activity, it's a local tradition that started spontaneously many years ago. There are plenty of middle-aged locals with special childhood memories of this market. With a look of nostalgia, they remember coming here with their parents to swap cards or look for a picture book, before having family *vermut* time.

St George's Day in Barcelona

According to bookseller Pablo, the book market is 'like celebrating Sant Jordi every week'. St George's Day on 23 April (known here as La Diada de Sant Jordi) is one of the most pleasant times of the year in Barcelona, when the streets and squares are filled with stalls selling roses and books. Traditionally, on this day boys give flowers to girls, and girls give books to boys. So for the locals, it's half Valentine's Day and half Book Day. However, this custom has been modified in modern times, with girls receiving books too, and families exchanging books with each other.

By Pablo Fernández Sopuerta
Pablo is a bookseller in Mercat Dominical de Sant Antoni. @mercatdominical santantoni

33 Getting Sweaty on MONTJUÏC

SCENERY | SPORT | RECREATION

Want to stay in shape while you're in Barcelona? Before grabbing a day pass to the local gym, consider working up a sweat on Montjuïc hill, which overlooks the city. It's also a favourite local spot for exercise, from yoga in the ancient Greek-style theatre to running or walking through the top attractions in the area.

ANOUCHKA/SHUTTERSTOCK ©

How to

Getting here From Paral·lel metro station, take the funicular railway to the upper station, Parc de Montjuïc. It's part of the metro fare system. Also the Telefèric del Port (Port Cable Car) connects La Barceloneta to Miramar station on Montjuïc.

When to go Year-round, but avoid exercising in hot weather during summer.

Tip Take water with you, as it's sometimes difficult to find kiosks that sell beverages. Also, wear comfortable shoes as it is hilly.

KYOKO KAWAGUCHI/LONELY PLANET ©

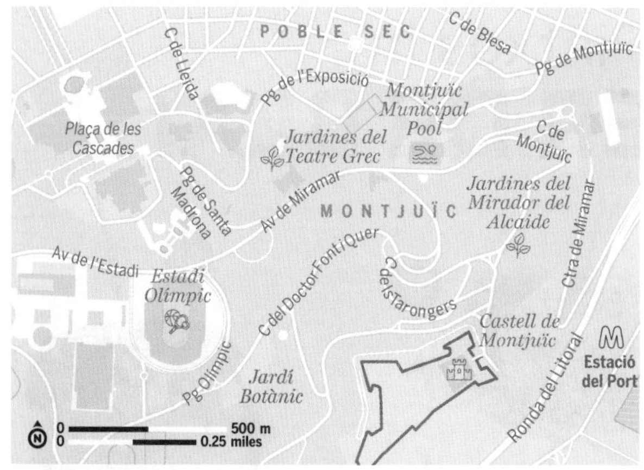

A Popular Local Exercise Spot

Slopes and stairs If you think a flat run along La Barceloneta seafront isn't enough, spice it up with slopes and stairs in **Montjuïc**. There are countless route options, but a loop covering the top highlights is good for killing two birds with one stone: sightseeing and exercise. From the **Parc de Montjuïc funicular station**, run up the slopes towards **Castell de Montjuïc**, keep going along the path overlooking the harbour, down to **Estadi Olímpic**, then continue past parks and museums, such as **Fundació Joan Miró** and **Museu Nacional d'Art de Catalunya**.

Tranquillity In the early morning, the hill is enveloped in silence, including **Jardines del Teatre Grec**, a garden easily accessible from the city centre, and **Jardines del Mirador del Alcaide**, another garden overlooking Barcelona. They are the perfect spots for morning yoga. Even in winter, thanks to the mild climate, you'll be in a T-shirt by the end of your routine.

Group classes There are all-level morning yoga classes in Spanish and English around **Jardines del Teatre Grec**. Laura Burbaite (yogaconlau.wixsite.com/yogaconlau) teaches on Saturdays and Mafe Prieto (somayogabcn.com) on Sundays. Mafe's classes are held at **Teatre Grec** except during colder months. For those who don't want to carry a mat around, mat rental is available for an additional fee if requested at the time of booking.

Left Montjuïc funicular **Below** Yoga at Montjuïc's Teatre Grec

Reward Yourself After a Workout

Why not recharge your energy before heading back to the city centre with a cold beverage or beer? If you happen to be there during the hottest season in Barcelona, visit the **Montjuïc Municipal Pool**, where some of the events of the 1992 Summer Olympics were held. Of course, you can take a dip in the cold water, but there is also a pool-side bar overlooking the city. It's just a stone's throw from the **Parc de Montjuïc funicular station**. Alternatively, a bar with exceptional views of the sea and the mountains, **La Caseta del Migdia**, is a 20-minute walk from the station.

Must-Eat Pintxos in
CARRER DE BLAI

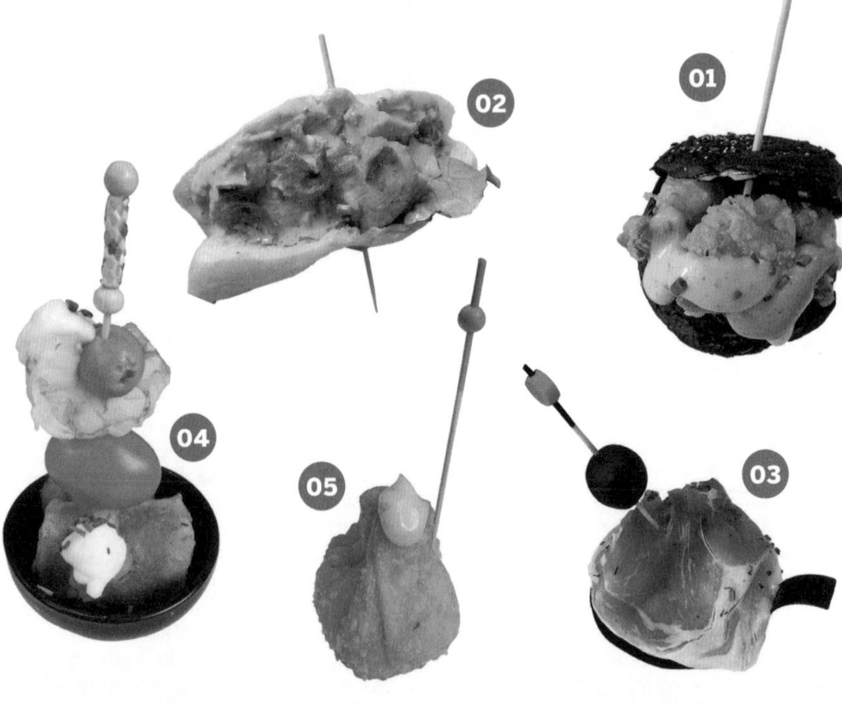

01

02

04

05

03

With Robert Albornoz
Robert is a huge fan of *pintxos* and organises La Ruta del Pincho, a stamp rally event of *pintxo* bars, @larutadelpincho

01 Squid Sandwich (La Tasqueta de Blai)
A striking contrast between crispy fried squid and soft black bread. Topped with mayonnaise and green onions.

02 Chicken Curry (La Tasqueta de Blai)
Indian-inspired, best with beer. Tender chicken dipped in creamy curry sauce served between soft bread.

03 Jamón Pancake (Blai 9)
Thin, soft pancakes topped with *jamón* (dry-cured ham) and black olives. The hidden flavours of tomato and coriander are refreshing.

04 Black Rice Roll (Blai 9)
Chinese fusion. A spring roll served with a prawn, an olive and mayonnaise.

05 Chicken Bag with Mustard and Honey Sauce (La Esquinita de Blai)
A bag of surprises. When you bite into the crispy empanada dough, chicken in a mustard-and-honey sauce will flood into your mouth.

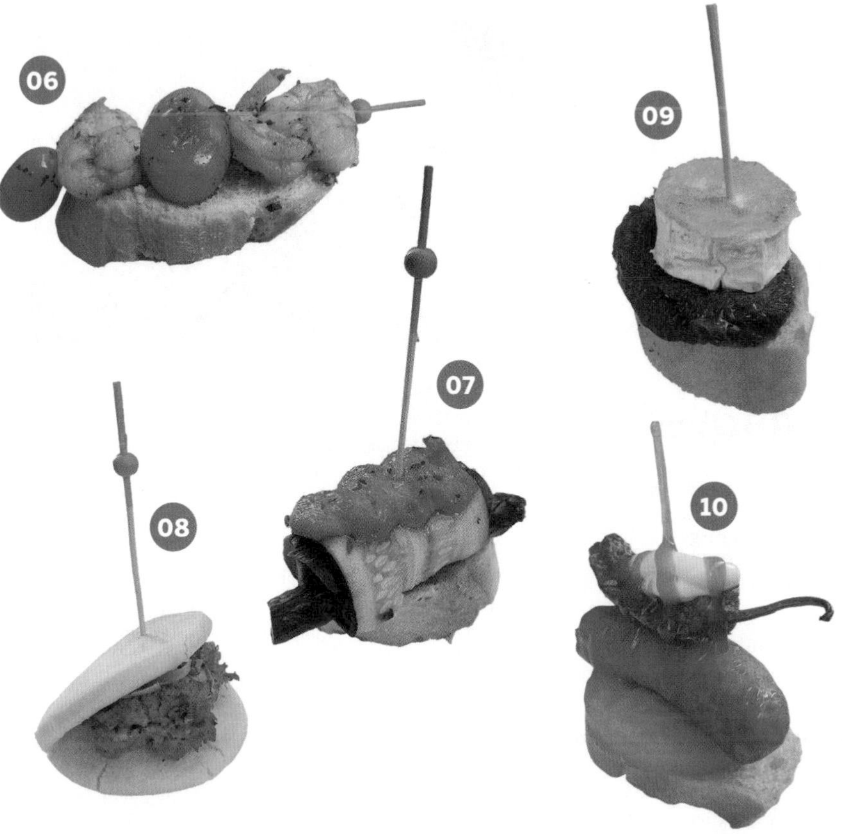

06 Prawn Brochette (La Esquinita de Blai)

Simple but tempting. Prawn with a rich, intense flavour and refreshing tomato with a hint of parsley and garlic.

07 Asparagus Roll (La Tiza)

Vegan. Crispy asparagus and caramelised onions rolled in a slice of zucchini. Topped with tomato sauce for an exceptional taste.

08 Bao Bun Pulled Pork (La Tiza)

American-Chinese inspired. Pulled pork stuffed in a *bao* (Chinese-style bun). The flavours are enhanced with coriander and pickled onions.

09 Goat's Cheese With Dried Tomatoes (La Bota Bar)

Queso de cabra (goat's cheese), a speciality of Catalan cuisine, combined with dried tomatoes. Simple yet flavoursome *pintxo.*

10 Chorizo with Padrón Peppers (La Bota Bar)

High-quality chorizo meets *pimiento de Padrón,* mildly bitter little peppers. The mellow mayonnaise is a secret ingredient that complements the other parts of the dish.

Five Mistakes in Eating Pa Amb Tomàquet

LEARN THE SECRET TECHNIQUES OF THE CATALAN PEOPLE

Pa amb tomàquet (bread with tomato) is a Catalan staple – tomato spread on a slice of bread seasoned with extra virgin olive oil and salt; raw garlic is optional. Almost every bar and restaurant in Barcelona serves this dish and, according to Catalans, there are closely guarded techniques on how to enjoy this dish properly.

Left Classic *pa amb tomàquet* **Middle** Tomatoes, La Boqueria market **Right** Sitting down to a *pa amb tomàquet* breakfast

Some eateries in Barcelona serve the ready-to-eat version of *pa amb tomàquet*. Others provide guests with the ingredients, such as whole tomatoes, bread and oil, so you can prepare it yourself to accompany your sausages, ham or cheese. It's just bread and tomato – sounds easy, right? Well, because of its simplicity, foreigners often end up eating it by 'freestyling', and there are plenty of pitfalls in preparing this classic Catalan dish.

1. Cutting in the wrong direction The moment I applied my knife to a tomato to make my very first *pa amb tomàquet*, I heard a scream from a Catalan friend saying 'Nooooooooo!' I was about to cut the tomato vertically, with its stalk end up. According to my friend, it's better to cut it horizontally so that the juicy part of the tomato comes out more easily.

2. Applying too much pressure After cutting it in the correct direction, I heard a second scream while rubbing the tomato against the bread. Another lesson: it's better to apply gentle but firm enough pressure to squeeze out mostly the juicy part, not the whole pulp.

3. Eating the skin So I set the tomato paste on the bread with oil and salt and devoured it with a sense of accomplishment. The skin of the tomato was left on the plate, but as it's edible, I put it in my mouth without thinking. Then I realised that my Catalan companions were regarding me oddly. As I shifted my gaze to their plates, I discovered that they don't eat the skins: they throw them away.

4. Freestyling before trying the basics Also, there have been several sightings of travellers inventing their own ways of eating *pa amb tomàquet*. One of my Catalan

OMERSUKRUGOKSU/GETTY IMAGES ©

CARACTERDESIGN/GETTY IMAGES ©

friends told me that she saw a foreigner eating it with vinegar instead of oil. Another friend saw a guy making a sliced tomato open sandwich with the provided ingredients. Well, enjoying the meal is the most essential part. Still, perhaps they should have avoided startling the locals and instead taken the opportunity to taste the magical, savoury flavour of the original version.

5. Choosing the wrong tomatoes You might like to try making *pa amb tomàquet* if you have access to a kitchen in your accommodation. You can buy the ingredients from the local market, but don't pick random tomatoes. Buy *tomàquets de penjar* (hanging tomatoes), which are tied together with string to store at room temperature. This type of tomato has a thinner skin, softer texture and more intense flavour, and leaves you with paper-thin skins after squeezing.

> It's just bread and tomato – sounds easy, right?

Keep in mind that there are many recipes and methods for preparing this dish. This may not be the definitive version, but it's a good start. *Bon profit* (bon appetit)!

Pa Amb Tomàquet Variations

Although there are various theories, many researchers have suggested *pa amb tomàquet* was originally invented to soften the texture of hard, dry bread with the juice of a tomato. Today, you can find restaurants serving this dish not only in Catalonia but also all over Spain. However, it seems that non-Catalan Spaniards also invent their own interpretations, perhaps because of the apparent simplicity of the dish. When visiting Seville or Madrid, a local newspaper reports that many Catalans are shocked to be served grated or pureed tomatoes with bread, which is a far cry from the original version.

Listings

BEST OF THE REST

Pintxo Bars on Carrer de Blai

La Tasqueta de Blai — €
One of the most popular bars on the street, with a laid-back atmosphere. The bite-sized lemon cream pie is the perfect dessert to round off bar-hopping along this street.

Blai 9 — €
With its picturesque and creative appearance and delightfully unique skewers, it would not be wrong to call these *pintxos* an art form. Some are served with pancakes instead of the standard bread.

La Esquinita de Blai — €
A cosy bar specialising in Basque-style *pintxos*. Tapas, burgers and salads are also available for those who want a larger portion.

La Tiza — €
This bar offers a unique experience while eating *pintxos*. As the name of the bar (which means chalk) suggests, there is a blackboard where you can doodle. Good for family gatherings and meeting friends.

La Bota Bar — €
Decorated with colourful objects, creating an artistic atmosphere. Classic black-and-white movies are shown, and sometimes live music is performed. Argentinian-style empanadas are the speciality.

Tapas & Aperitifs around Calle Parlament

Bar Alegría — €€
Established in 1899, this bar with an antique ambience has recently been reopened. In addition to the classic tapas, the 'bikinis' (ham-and-cheese grilled sandwiches) are popular among the locals.

Cuina de Barri — €€
Stylish and simple restaurant. Tapas and typical Mediterranean dishes with a modern, creative touch. The set lunch menu is a good deal.

Bar Calders — €€
Popular aperitif spot, always packed with locals. The menu offers a wide variety of snacks, from Mediterranean to Mexican dishes. The spacious terrace is a great place to enjoy a sunny day.

Bar i Cafeteria Masclans Orígens — €€
A tapas bar inside the Mercat de Sant Antoni specialising in *bacalao* (Atlantic cod). Order it fried with savoury tomato sauce while enjoying the lively atmosphere of the market.

Restaurant Sucursal Aceitera — €€€
Spacious, bright dining area serving elaborate tapas, lunch and dinner. The sunny terrace space is always full of regulars eating the set lunch menu.

Coffee & Breakfast/Brunch

Café Cometa — €€
A warm and welcoming space with high ceilings and wooden furniture. In the morning it quickly fills up with locals looking for homemade pastries, sandwiches and quality coffee.

Cohen Taberna — €€
With its relaxing white-themed interior, this is the perfect spot for brunch or a light meal, or quiet afternoon reading. For those with a sweet tooth, the carrot cake with fresh-cheese frosting is a must-try.

Syra Coffee – Poble Sec — €
A simple takeaway coffee shop with several locations in Barcelona. Its freshly roasted single-origin coffee, made by knowledgeable

baristas, is highly regarded by local coffee connoisseurs.

Federal Café €€

Famous for its hipster atmosphere. Also popular as a working cafe among locals. Start the day with the avocado toast while basking in the sunshine streaming in through the large windows.

Quick Bites

La Pizza del Sortidor Poble Sec €€

Authentic Italian-style pizza restaurant in a small square with outside seats. The dough is baked in a wood-fired oven. Some locals say it's one of the best pizzas in Barcelona.

Fish and Chips Shop €€

Small bar near Rocafort metro station. People line up at night for freshly fried fish covered with extra-crunchy breading and special seasonings. Sweet-potato fries are another favourite.

Urban Parks & Views

Jardins de les Tres Xemeneies

The three chimneys of the old power station are local landmarks. Every Saturday, there's a slow-food eco farmers' market, where you can buy artisanal and seasonal products.

Jardins de Càndida Pérez

A quiet little park behind the library near the Mercat de Sant Antoni. It's a great place to relax or to let the kids play after a long day walking around the city.

Arenas de Barcelona

An old bullring turned into a modern shopping centre. The open-air top floor, which has a lot of bars and restaurants, is one of the best places to view the whole of Plaça d'Espanya.

Parque del Mirador del Poble Sec

Another hidden spot to enjoy the views over the city. Located between Montjuïc and the

Museo Olímpico y de Deportes Juan Antonio Samaranch

Poble Sec neighbourhood. There are children's playgrounds and shady trees.

Montjuïc Museums & Architecture

CaixaForum Barcelona

The art museum hosts not only various art exhibitions but also concerts and shows. The building is a former modernist textile factory designed by Josep Puig i Cadafalch, an important Modernista architect.

Mies van der Rohe Pavilion

A must-see spot for design and architecture lovers. A reconstruction of the German Pavilion from 1929's Barcelona International Exhibition, designed by Ludwig Mies van der Rohe and Lilly Reich.

Museo Olímpico y de Deportes Juan Antonio Samaranch

Sports-themed museum right next to the Olympic Stadium. The collection includes costumes and shoes of Spanish Olympic athletes.

DAY TRIPS

WINE | BEACHES | MEDIEVAL HISTORY

DAY TRIPS
Trip Builder

ESCAPE FROM THE CITY

Everybody knows the modernist city of Barcelona but, with over 740 kilometres of coastline, a prominent medieval past and a deeply rooted wine culture, Catalonia is a wonderful land filled with world-class sights, many of them easily reached on a day trip from Barcelona.

Trip Notes

Best for Beach, wine, rural towns, culture.

Transport Cities are well connected by either train or bus. A car is needed for the smaller towns.

Getting around By foot in cities, but a car or motorcycle for village-hopping is a must.

Tip Avoid taking day trips on weekends.

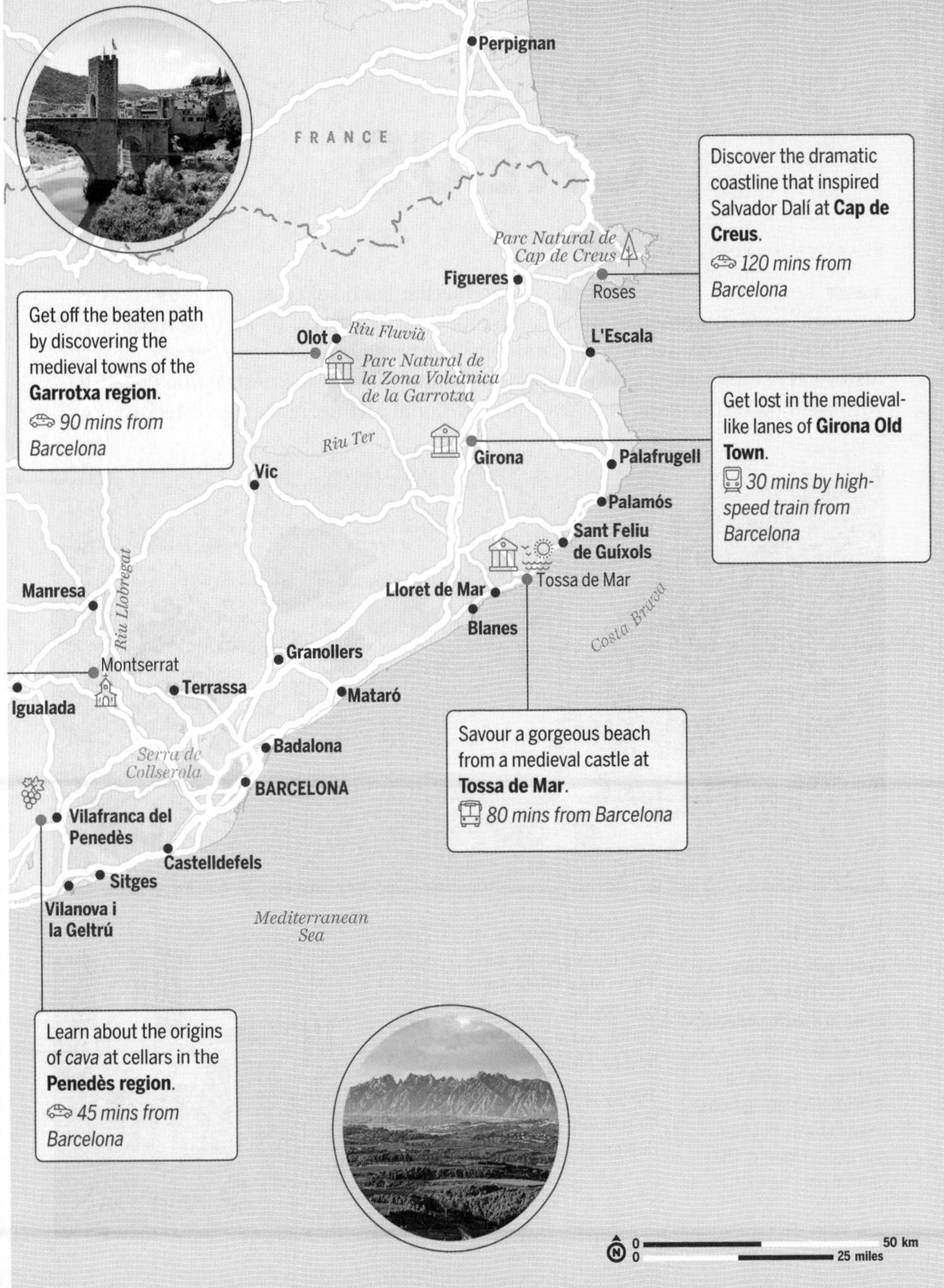

Perpignan
FRANCE
Discover the dramatic coastline that inspired Salvador Dalí at **Cap de Creus**.
120 mins from Barcelona
Parc Natural de Cap de Creus
Figueres
Roses
Get off the beaten path by discovering the medieval towns of the **Garrotxa region**.
90 mins from Barcelona
Olot
Riu Fluvià
Parc Natural de la Zona Volcànica de la Garrotxa
L'Escala
Get lost in the medieval-like lanes of **Girona Old Town**.
30 mins by high-speed train from Barcelona
Riu Ter
Girona
Palafrugell
Vic
Palamós
Sant Feliu de Guíxols
Tossa de Mar
Lloret de Mar
Blanes
Manresa
Riu Llobregat
Costa Brava
Granollers
Montserrat
Terrassa
Igualada
Mataró
Savour a gorgeous beach from a medieval castle at **Tossa de Mar**.
80 mins from Barcelona
Badalona
Serra de Collserola
BARCELONA
Vilafranca del Penedès
Castelldefels
Sitges
Vilanova i la Geltrú
Mediterranean Sea
Learn about the origins of *cava* at cellars in the **Penedès region**.
45 mins from Barcelona
0 50 km
0 25 miles

34 Cap de CREUS

BEACHES, NATURE, DALÍ

Located on the eastern side of the Iberian Peninsula, Cap de Creus is a natural park composed of lunar landscapes, vertiginous cliffs and the most breathtaking coastal scenery in Catalonia. The area also contains a set of historical fishing villages, which are now wonderful touristic destinations packed with seafood restaurants, beaches and traditional Mediterranean architecture.

AMAZING TRAVELS/SHUTTERSTOCK ©

How to

Getting there Catch a train to Figueres and then a bus to Roses, Cadaqués or Port de la Selva.

Getting around A car is helpful for going from town to town, but you can explore part of the natural park on foot.

When to go Summer is best for swimming, but it gets busy. Winters are cold but free of crowds. Spring and autumn are best for hiking.

Tip If you have to choose one village, go to Cadaqués.

BEARFOTOS/SHUTTERSTOCK ©

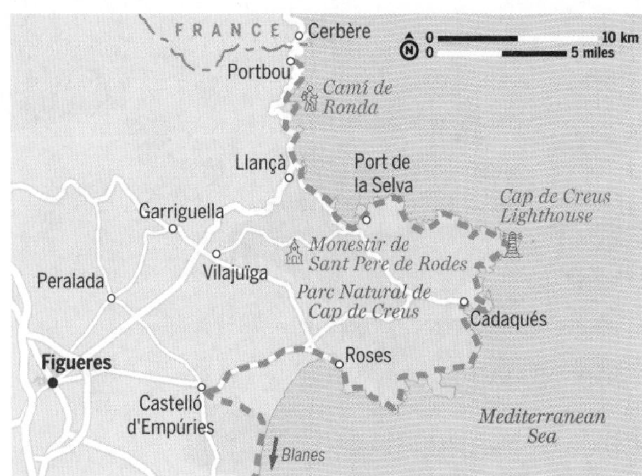

Hiking along Camí de Ronda Camí de Ronda is a hiking trail that goes along the edge of Costa Brava, from the town of Blanes to the French border. Walking along this gorgeous trail is the best way to experience the allure and magic of the natural park. Day trippers can do the 7km walk from Cadaqués to Cap de Creus lighthouse, down Spain's eastern coast. Fit travellers with more time should attempt the hike from Roses to Cadaqués (18km), which goes through absolutely unspoilt hidden coves and pine forests. Pack lunch because there's almost nothing in between.

Salvador Dalí and Cap de Creus Born in the nearby city of Figueres, the surrealist painter visited Cap de Creus from childhood, a dazzling setting that truly inspired him throughout his life. Many of his paintings, including *The Great Masturbator,* have been either inspired by or are filled with allegories from these landscapes. In 1930, Dalí moved with Gal.la to Cadaqués, where they lived until she died in 1982. Today, his former surrealist house has become a museum that showcases the painter's life through all those decades. Tickets (€14) can be bought on the official website. You should note, however, that this museum doesn't display Dalí's significant works. For these, you should visit Museu Dalí in Figueres.

Left Camí de Ronda **Bottom left** Monestir de Sant Pere de Rodes

Monestir de Sant Pere de Rodes

If you had to visit one place outside of Barcelona, it should be Monestir de Sant Pere de Rodes, a 9th-century Benedictine monastery. An outstanding piece of Catalan Romanesque architecture, the monastery overlooks the rugged coastline of Cap de Creus. Today an official starting point for the Camino de Santiago, the monastery had been a prominent pilgrimage point for centuries, but sackings, pirates and plagues brought it to near ruin in the 17th century. Its magnificent location and architecture, nonetheless, are reason enough to attract visitors. The monastery houses a restaurant that serves traditional Catalan food. Book in advance.

By Robin Townsend, *photojournalist and historian, @robin_townsend*

35 Cheers to PRIORAT

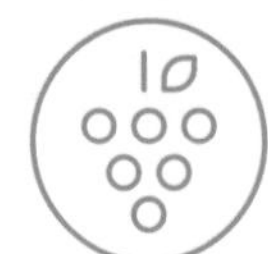

WINE, VILLAGES, OFF THE BEATEN PATH

Ancient, family-owned wineries, visually appealing villages and attractive stepped vineyards, the region of Priorat offers visitors the opportunity to experience the most authentic and romantic side of wine. The cherry on top is that its cellars produce some of the most sophisticated wines in the country.

JOE BECERRA/SHUTTERSTOCK ©

How to

Getting there Take a train to Marçà-Falset (two hours).

Getting around A car is needed to move between villages.

Harvest season Wine regions are best visited during harvest. In Priorat, it runs between mid-August and the end of September, depending on vineyard location.

Local tip Plan your itinerary based on the wineries you visit, but book two or three days in advance at least.

IVANABRAMKIN/SHUTTERSTOCK ©

The Perfect Road Trip

The mountainous landscape of Priorat is dotted with unquestionably alluring, charming villages. Start your trip in **Porrera**, home to some of Priorat's oldest wineries. Next stop should be **Siurana**, the most touristy town in Priorat, which is built over a cliff with mind-blowing views. Continue driving to **Escaladei**, where you can visit the medieval Cartoixa, and **La Vilella Baixa**, known as the Manhattan of Priorat for its nine-storey buildings, quite impressive for a village of fewer than 300 people. **Gratallops** is worth a visit too, holding perhaps the largest concentration of cellars. Finish your road trip in **Falset**, the regional capital.

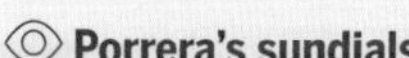

Porrera's sundials

Visitors often wonder about the 14 sundials found throughout the 400-inhabitant village of Porrera. These beautiful sundials, all of them different, were built between 1840 and 1880 to show the economic splendour Porrera was enjoying.

ETTENAEJ/SHUTTERSTOCK ©

Top left A hillside Priorat vineyard
Left Porrera **Above** Gratallops

DOQ Priorat and DO Montsant Priorat is a tiny Catalan region that belongs to Tarragona province, where two Denominaciones de Origen (DO) – Appellations of Origin – are produced: DOQ Priorat and DO Montsant. DOQ Priorat, the Q standing for Qualified for having a matchless quality, is exclusively produced within the region of Priorat, where the vineyards are typically placed on steep gradients. On the other hand, Montsant is produced in the neighbouring region of Ribera d'Ebre, with the grapes grown on flatter land.

Visiting a winery Nobody can leave Priorat without visiting a few wine cellars, not only to taste the exclusive wines but also to experience the daily life of a traditional winery, where a significant part of the work is still done manually. For a more authentic experience, visit a small winery, producing no more than a few thousand bottles a year. But don't miss the bigger cellars, since they will likely have a larger variety of wines to taste. Check

Top Tipples

Priorat houses more than 90 wine cellars. Wineries with DOQ or DO are a certificate of excellence, so you can never go wrong.

Álvaro Palacios (DOQ Priorat) Best-known winery, a fame gained for producing some of the finest wines in the region.

Celler de Capçanes (DO Montsant) Known for its Kosher wines.

Bodega Celler Burgos Porta (DOQ Priorat) A 19th-century family-owned winery specialising in organic wines.

Mas Doix (DOQ Priorat) Renowned, award-winning wine cellar.

Hericamps (DOQ Priorat) Small winery producing 5000 bottles a year.

Left Álvaro Palacios winery
Below Cartoixa d'Escaladei monastery

the tourism board's website (turismepriorat.org/en/wine-holidays-priorat), where you can filter the distinct wineries by attributes like DO, type of production or number of bottles.

Oleoturismo Just like with wine, in Priorat you may also enjoy olive oil tasting, locally referred to as *oleoturismo* (oil tourism). This area is well known for the quality of its olives and, in the municipality of Cabacés, the family Miró Cubells offers visits to their *molí,* where you can witness the artisanal way of making olive oil, as well as tasting the distinct varieties. Locals typically eat the oil with bread, cheese and *jamón.*

Cartoixa d'Escaladei In the locality of Escaladei, there is a 12th-century monastery founded by Carthusian monks who, over a period of 700 years, contributed enormously to the development of Priorat, including the region's viticulture. It's partially restored, and visitors can wonder around the cloister, church, courtyards and monks' rooms. The entrance fee is €5 and guided visits in English are available.

The Heroic Viticulture of Priorat Wine Region

A REGION WHERE WINE IS PRODUCED TRADITIONALLY

Spain has 69 Denominaciones de Origen (DO) – Appellations of Origin – but only two of them have achieved the premium status of DOQ, a category assigned to wines of outstanding quality. One of them is Rioja, and the other is Priorat, a tiny wine region known for its traditional and heroic viticulture.

Left Harvesting grapes **Middle** Display at a Priorat winery **Right** A characteristically rugged Priorat vineyard

XAVITGN/SHUTTERSTOCK ©

Undeniably, the Catalan wine region of Priorat produces some of the best wines in Spain. Yet, they tend to be a rare find on most restaurant menus and supermarket shelves, which typically favour Riojas, Riberas del Duero or Penedès. No, it's not a matter of bad marketing, but the topography of Priorat makes wine production extremely challenging: the area's rugged, steep hills form spectacular mountainous amphitheaters, with vineyards often placed on 50% inclination slopes, locally named *costers*.

Even with today's technology, the grape harvest in Priorat is essentially manual. Come during the season and you are likely to witness harvesters walking among those steep gradients with gloves and a big bucket hanging from their backs, exactly like their grandparents used to do 60 or 70 years ago. The terrain and Priorat's poor soil, mainly formed of numerous layers of *llicorella*, a type of slate that doesn't retain any water, make wine production in Priorat particularly limited, but of very high quality.

The Concept of Heroic Viticulture

There is, however, a bright side to this story. Such territorial conditions have made Priorat a wine region with a strong personality that has managed to retain the romanticism that has always typified the consumption of wine, an attribute that is being diluted by mechanisation and industrialisation elsewhere. There isn't a lot of space for vines in these lands, so you won't find monster corporations here. Rather, you'll experience traditional and family-owned cellars, many of them located in *masos* (traditional Catalan farmhouses), with plenty of secrets and stories to tell, all part of Priorat's historical heritage and its heroic viticulture.

DAVID SILVERMAN/GETTY IMAGES ©

PUYALROYO/SHUTTERSTOCK ©

Over the last few years, DOQ Priorat has put tremendous effort into preserving and adding value to its unique and historical wine heritage. DOQ Priorat wines are classified into five strata, a pyramid the different wines can climb depending on a wide variety of factors, ranging from the age of the vines to the vineyard inclination and historical background. These elements define the concept of heroic viticulture.

Over the last few years, DOQ Priorat has put tremendous effort into preserving and adding value to its unique and historical wine heritage.

Cartoixa d'Escaladei

Visitors often wonder why anyone would start growing vines in such difficult terrain but back in the 12th century a group of Carthusian monks from Provence (in today's France) arrived in the region of Priorat. They founded a monastery named Cartoixa d'Escaladei, bringing along their knowledge and techniques, which they used for developing a viticulture that took root in the area. Over the following decades, and for seven centuries, these monks acquired the jurisdiction and control of all the villages that later became the region of Priorat.

However, with the Spanish Confiscation of Mendiazábal in 1836, the grape phylloxera of 1855, and the subsequently growing textile industry absorbing all the workforce, that beautiful wine culture experienced a huge decline. It's only been since the 1980s that, thanks to the excellent work of the farmers from Priorat, boosted by the local administration's resources, the wine industry began to flourish again.

Old vineyards often have great stories waiting to be unveiled. Mas de la Rosa was one of the first *mas* (farmhouses) in Porrera to make wine. The local legend says that in the mid-18th century, the wife of a former owner went mad and burnt the house to the ground, probably as an act of rebellion. She was never seen again, but her name was forevermore linked to the *mas*. Today, we produce our most exclusive wine, named Mas de la Rosa, from this estate, a 1.9-hectare vineyard with 80-year-old vines planted on steep slopes, somehow keeping alive Rosa's intriguing tale.

Told by Miguel Torres Maczassek, *fifth generation of Familia Torres*

36 Medieval GARROTXA

ARCHITECTURE | CULTURE | VILLAGES

Garrotxa is a region in Girona province dotted with ancient villages that, thanks to centuries of isolation and rooted local traditions, have managed to preserve their former essence and medieval architecture. Hopping from village to village while savouring local specialities like *butifarra de perol amb mongetes* (traditional pork sausage with white beans) is an experience not to be missed.

Trip Notes

Getting there Teisa buses run daily from Pau Claris 117 (Barcelona) to the town of Besalú.

Getting around A car is needed for moving between villages.

Where to eat For an authentic Catalan culinary experience, go to Can Bundancia.

Itinerary add-ons Fageda d'en Jordà is an exceptionally beautiful beech forest. While technically not part of Garrotxa, the villages of Rupit (Osona) and Beget (Ripollès) are worth a visit.

La Catalunya Profunda

Literally translating as 'Deep Catalonia', La Catalunya Profunda refers to the interior, rural regions of Catalonia, composed of the towns and villages with the strongest Catalan identity, like Garrotxa. In these areas, Spanish is rarely spoken and pro-independence symbols are raised on the top of every bell tower.

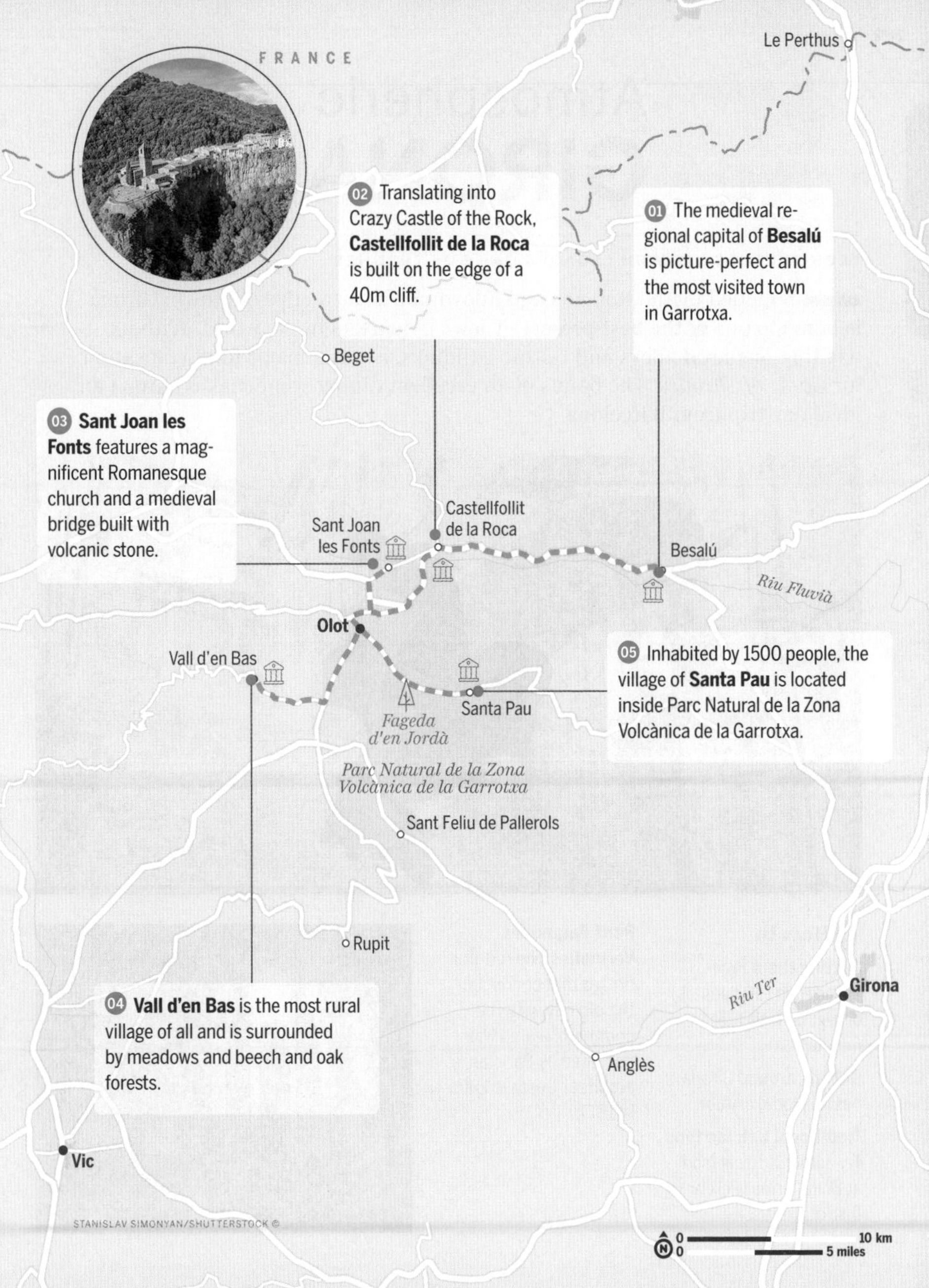
FRANCE
Le Perthus
02 Translating into Crazy Castle of the Rock, **Castellfollit de la Roca** is built on the edge of a 40m cliff.
01 The medieval regional capital of **Besalú** is picture-perfect and the most visited town in Garrotxa.
Beget
03 **Sant Joan les Fonts** features a magnificent Romanesque church and a medieval bridge built with volcanic stone.
Castellfollit de la Roca
Sant Joan les Fonts
Besalú
Riu Fluvià
Olot
Vall d'en Bas
05 Inhabited by 1500 people, the village of **Santa Pau** is located inside Parc Natural de la Zona Volcànica de la Garrotxa.
Santa Pau
Fageda d'en Jordà
Parc Natural de la Zona Volcànica de la Garrotxa
Sant Feliu de Pallerols
Rupit
Riu Ter
Girona
04 **Vall d'en Bas** is the most rural village of all and is surrounded by meadows and beech and oak forests.
Anglès
Vic
0 10 km
0 5 miles

37 Atmospheric GIRONA

ARCHITECTURE | JEWISH LEGACY | GAME OF THRONES

Founded by the Romans and known for its attractive old town, Girona is home to one of the best-preserved Jewish quarters in the world. With its winding medieval alleys and Gothic buildings, it was a major filming location for *Game of Thrones*. The bonus of an excellent dining scene makes Girona an ideal day trip from Barcelona.

DEYAN DENCHEV/SHUTTERSTOCK ©

How to

Getting there High-speed train (30 minutes) or regular train (75 minutes).

Getting around Girona is best explored on foot.

Traditional Catalan food Try authentic local food at Boira, Arròs i Peix or Le Bistrot.

Pont Palanques Vermelles The red-iron bridge that connects the old city with the commercial area was designed by Parisian architect Gustave Eiffel in 1877.

UNAI HUIZI PHOTOGRAPHY/SHUTTERSTOCK ©

El Call Jueu de Girona Call is the Catalan way of saying Jewish Quarter, which comes from the Hebrew word *khalal.* Jews inhabited the winding alleys of the old city until 1492, when the Spanish Inquisition expelled them from their kingdoms, in an attempt to keep their Catholic orthodoxy. Today, the former synagogue has become the Museu d'Història dels Jueus, which tells the history of Jewish communities in Catalonia and their crucial role in the country's development, with a strong focus on the Jews who lived in the call.

Girona Game of Thrones self-guided walking tour Once you are in the old city, go up the 90 steps that Cersei Lannister climbed with the cry of 'Shame..., Shame..., Shame...' and that lead to the imposing Girona Cathedral that was blown up by the green Wildfire. Then, follow the steps of Arya Stark at Carrer del Bisbe Josep Cartanà, the street where she was wandering blindly. When Arya was chased by The Waif, she entered the 12th-century Arab Baths, until she was eventually stabbed at Pujada de Sant Domènec, shortly after contemplating the enormous statue of Braavos from Pere de Galligants bridge. Plaça dels Jurats (Braavor Theater), Ferran el Catòlic street (Braavos market) and Monestir de Sant Pere de Galligants (King's Landing Cloister) were other filming locations.

Left Girona's evocative old town
Bottom left Arab baths

The Roca Universe in Girona

Opened in 1986 by the Roca brothers, Celler de Can Roca is a three-Michelin-star restaurant that offers creative Catalan cuisine. It's considered one of the best restaurants in the world. A meal at Celler de Can Roca requires a lot of money and several months of waiting for your booking date to come round. Alternatively, you can have lunch at Can Roca, a local eatery run by the brothers' parents and serving homemade meals. The sweet-toothed should also try the ice-cream sandwiches at Rocambolesc and taste the chocolates from Casa Cacao, both of which are run by the same brothers.

Practicalities

Right Barcelona's Arc de Triomf

EASY STEPS FROM THE AIRPORT TO THE CITY CENTRE

Barcelona International Airport (Josep Tarradellas Barcelona – el Prat) is the most common entry point for travellers visiting Barcelona. Long-distance flights operate at Terminal 1, while low-budget and EU flights use Terminals 1 and 2. Restaurants, shops, and all services are available in both terminals, but Terminal 1 is bigger and newer. You may also fly into Reus or Girona airports.

AT THE AIRPORT

SIM CARD
Orange and Vodafone pre-paid SIM cards are sold at Tech&Fly (Terminals 1 and 2) and Tabacs (Terminal 1). Shops open from 6.30am to 10pm. At the time of writing, it wasn't possible to buy one after closing time due to COVID-19.

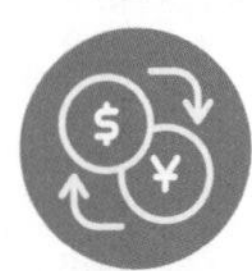

INTERNATIONAL CURRENCY EXCHANGE
Always open Global Exchange stalls are scattered around both terminals, but the exchange rates offered are poor. It is recommended to bring euros (€) from your home country, or exchange currency at the banks in the city. Credit cards can be used anywhere.

VENIAMIN KRASKOV/SHUTTERSTOCK ©

WI-FI Free, unlimited wi-fi is available throughout the airport. Connect to Airport Free Wi-Fi AENA.

ATMS Caixabank, Bankia and Euronet ATMs are available in both terminals.

CHARGING STATIONS There are no charging stations at the arrivals hall, just occasional, random wall sockets.

CUSTOMS REGULATIONS

Duty free Less than 200 cigarettes, 1L of alcoholic beverages more than 22%, 2L of alcoholic beverages less than 22%, 4L of wine and 16L of beer.

Tax & refunds Non-EU citizens are entitled to a 21% tax refund on some goods; ask for DIVA tax-free form at the time of purchase.

GETTING TO THE CITY CENTRE

Aerobús The airport shuttle bus runs every 15 minutes to the city centre (Plaça Catalunya), plus three stops in between. Catch it just outside the arrivals hall at each terminal. Tickets can be purchased from the machines or staff at the bus stop. The trip takes about 35 minutes and costs €5.90.

Train Renfe operates from Terminal 2 to Barcelona Sants (main train station) and Passeig de Gràcia (downtown). The station is five minutes away from the arrivals hall, just over the bridge. Trains depart every 30 minutes; 20-25 minutes, €2.40 (for either station).

Metro Line 9 runs from Terminals 1 and 2 to the city centre, with transfers at Torrassa (Line 1), Collblanc (Line 5) and Zona Universitària (Line 3). There are departures every seven minutes. The trip takes about 45 minutes and costs €5.15 (any stop).

HOW MUCH FOR A...

Taxi Pick-up area is outside the arrivals hall (both terminals). It's a 20- to 30-minute trip to the city centre. Taxis accept credit cards.

Night bus N16 (Terminal 2), N17 (Terminal 1) and N18 (Terminals 1 and 2) run between the airport and city centre (€2.40) at night.

Further information For the train, you can purchase a T-Casual (€11.35), an individual ticket worth 10 journeys that's also valid for city metro and bus.

Aerobús Runs 5.30am to 1am.

Metro Runs 5am to midnight (2am on Friday and Saturday).

Train Runs from 5.30am to 11.30pm.

Outside of the above times, only night buses or taxis are available.

OTHER POINTS OF ENTRY

Estació del Nord Bus station with direct connections to several European cities in France, Andorra, Italy, Romania, Germany, Switzerland, Portugal, Ukraine and Poland, as well as all major cities in Spain. The station is located 1.5km from Plaça Catalunya.

Estació de Sants Main rail station in Barcelona, with direct connections to most major Spanish cities like Valencia and Madrid, and also European cities like Paris and Milan.

Inbound ferries Arrive at Terminal de Creuers Port de Barcelona. There are seven cruise terminals and the Cruise Bus operates between them and Monument a Colón (end of La Rambla). Fare is €3. Going by foot is also possible, up to 2km, depending on the terminal.

Girona International Airport Located 90km from Barcelona city centre. Line 602 connects the airport with Barcelona Estació del Nord (75 minutes) with departures every 20 to 25 minutes. Buses run until 9pm. After that, taxis are available.

Reus International Airport Situated 103km from the city centre. Direct buses (€16) operate from the airport to Sant Estació.

TRANSPORT TIPS TO HELP YOU GET AROUND

TMB

Transports Metropolitans de Barcelona (tmb.cat/en) is the official site for metro and bus information.

METRO

With 12 lines, the metro is the quickest and most convenient way to get around. Different integrated ticket options and fares are available.

A single metro ticket
€2.40

Children under four travel free

Get your map from the TMB mobile app

WALKING

The city's relatively compact size allows travellers to go neighbourhood-hopping and reach most landmarks on foot.

CITY BUS

Convenient when your metro line doesn't have a direct connection, or during off hours. Tickets must be purchased inside the metro stations. Same fares apply.

TAXIS

Licensed yellow taxis can be taken all across the city. The basic fare is €2.25, increasing €1.18 per kilometre during the day and €1.41 at night. All taxis accept credit cards. When it comes to taxi apps, FREE NOW is popular, with slightly lower fares than regular taxis. Taxi Ecològic is a local company that only operates with low-emission vehicles.

TRAM

Three available lines, running between different sections of Avinguda Diagonal. Useful if you're staying in the area, but not for linking major sights.

BICYCLE

With 200km of bike lanes, it's safe and easy to get around Barcelona by bicycle. Note that the public bicycle service (Bicing) is only available to residents.

TIP Integrated tickets are valid when changing between metro and bus within a 70-minute window. Does not apply to single tickets.

Left Buying metro tickets
TUPUNGATO/SHUTTERSTOCK ©

ACCESSIBILITY

Public transport in Barcelona is highly accessible for those with restricted mobility. All buses come with an access ramp and reserved seats for passengers with disabilities. The metro network is sight and wheelchair accessible, with lifts at all but 14 of the 162 stations. The city council is currently working on making improvements to accessibility for vision-impaired travellers. Further details are available at tmb.cat/en/barcelona/accessibility-mobility-reduced.

PUBLIC TRANSPORT ESSENTIALS

Tickets Metro, bus and tram systems work with the same travel card, which can be purchased at metro and tram stations (not bus stations).

Metro opening hours The metro runs from 5am to midnight Sunday to Thursday; and 5am to 2am on Friday, Saturday and the day before a public holiday.

Hola Barcelona Travel card that provides unlimited journeys (metro, bus and tram) for consecutive periods (two, three, four and five days) from the time you purchase it. The card is non-transferable and can only be purchased online (holabarcelona.com/tickets/hola-bcn-barcelona-travel-card).

Barcelona Bus Turístic Official hop-on, hop-off bus that takes you through Barcelona's most popular landmarks. General price is €30, but reduced fares apply. Buy your tickets on the official website (holabarcelona.com/tickets/barcelona-hop-on-hop-off-bus-tour).

Night bus There are 19 lines operating after metro closing hours. Same fares apply.

Ferrocarrils de la Generalitat (FGC) There are four metro lines that are not locally referred to as metro but FGC, mostly reaching the districts of Zona Alta, at the foot of the mountain of Collserola.

Zones Both metro and bus exclusively operate within Zone 1, but FGC runs between six different zones (with increasing fares applying to each).

Left Barcelona Bus Turístic **Top right** Glories metro station **Above** Ferrocarrils de la Generalitat

UNIQUE & LOCAL WAYS TO STAY

As one of the world's most visited cities, Barcelona offers a wide variety of hostels, boutique hotels and apartments, many located in historic buildings. The best area to stay will largely depend on your preferences and interests but, given the city's compact size, everything is relatively close.

Find a place to stay in Barcelona

BOUTIQUE HOTELS

With a limited number of rooms, boutique hotels offer guests a more cosy and intimate experience. In a city known for its medieval and modernist architecture, they often come with the added bonus of being located in historic buildings.

HOSTELS

From stylish, beautifully decorated hostels to party palaces offering pub crawls or bed and bikes, hostels are not just aimed at budget backpackers these days. They have evolved into a sophisticated travelling lifestyle choice, and Barcelona has plenty of variety on offer.

B&BS

B&B stays provide the enticing combination of a central location in chic, cushy apartments with a more local flavour that tends to be missed in hotel stays.

PISO TURÍSTICOS

Holiday apartments are the best value-for-money option for families and larger groups of travellers. Plus Spaniards love to cook, so having a fully equipped kitchen is guaranteed. From budget to luxury apartments and everything in between, the range here is limitless.

BOOKING

Booking several weeks ahead is recommended, especially if you're coming during the peak season of Easter, July and August, and Christmas holidays. For a slightly better rate, contact properties directly. Local booking sites include:

Barcelona 30 (barcelona30.com) Low-cost accommodation options (up to €40 per person per night), including hotels, hostels, apartments and B&Bs.

Oh-Barcelona (oh-barcelona.com) Popular for holiday apartment deals; also lists hotels.

WHERE TO STAY, IF YOU LOVE...

→**Beach, seafood & local life** Barceloneta & the Waterfront (p92) Great for sun-bathing, walking along the promenade and seafood tapas. For a more local experience, stay in Poblenou. There's only one metro line in the area.

Gaudí, dining scene & local markets La Sagrada Familia & L'Eixample (p112) A convenient district to set up base that's close to everything. Several modernist gems can be found here and you'll be spoilt for choice with dining options.

History, architecture & neighbourhood walks La Rambla & Barri Gòtic (p30) Ideal for learning about the city's Roman and medieval past. It's close to the beach and other sites of interest. Watch out for pickpockets and tourist traps.

Museums, cultural diversity & bars El Raval (p54) The most vibrant and multicultural district. Great for bar-hopping and close to Barri Gòtic and Sant Antoni. Nights can be noisy.

History, art & nightlife La Ribera (p72) Only a few minutes' walk from La Barceloneta and l'Eixample. Great international atmosphere and cocktail-bar scene.

↓**Local culture, eco-shopping & Gaudí** Gràcia & Park Güell (p136) Well connected to the city centre and great for hanging with locals. Plenty of bars to choose from.

Outdoors, high-end city life & football Camp Nou, Pedralbes & La Zona Alta (p156) Barcelona's wealthiest district, with loads of fine-dining options. In some areas, public transport is limited and accommodation can be pricey (except for Les Corts).

Local life, restaurants & museums Montjuïc, Poble Sec & Sant Antoni (p170) A local area within walking distance of the city centre. Plenty of gourmet places and bar terraces for *vermut*. Loads of museums and green areas in Montjuïc.

Previous page Hotel Oriente **Left** Meeting in Gràcia
Above Barceloneta beach

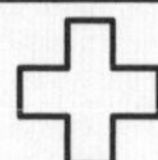

DANGERS, ANNOYANCES & SAFETY

Barcelona is popularly known as the pickpocket capital of Europe. Petty crime has become a major problem here and La Rambla and the streets of Barri Gòtic, El Raval and Barceloneta are filled with professional thieves waiting tourists.

DISTRACTIONS Thieves tend to act in groups, one of whom may try to distract you while the others take your valuables. Typical distractions include asking for directions with a map, falling over in front of you, dropping something, or even good-looking girls being overly nice. If you encounter such unusual behaviour, turn your back and walk away.

SNATCH-AND-GRAB While distractions mainly target tourists, thieves playing snatch-and-grab don't discriminate between locals and visitors. As a rule of thumb, never leave your phone on the table of a bar terrace. Similarly, if you need to use your phone when walking around La Rambla or Barceloneta, always hold it tightly. Also remember to never leave your belongings unattended on the beach.

REPORT A CRIME Going to the police won't help you recover your belongings, but it might be useful for insurance purposes. *Denuncia* is the Spanish word for police report, which you can make at any station of the Guàrdia Urbana (Barcelona police, Carrer Rambla 43) or Mossos d'Esquadra (Catalan police, Carrer Nou de la Rambla 76).

El Raval Recently, there have been reports of tourists getting mugged late at night (4am or 5am) in the streets of El Raval. While this shouldn't stop you from going there, avoid walking around the area at those hours.

SOPA IMAGES/GETTY IMAGES ©

DAVID RAMOS/GETTY IMAGES ©

Recreational drug use is not criminalised in Spain, but its consumption in public areas is subject to a fine.

MEDICAL SERVICES
As a foreigner, you have the right to receive medical emergency treatment for free, but your insurance should pay for any treatment beyond that. EU citizens must hold the European Health Insurance Card.

PHARMACIES
Pharmacies in Barcelona are plentiful. At night, ask for the *farmacia de guardia*, the only open pharmacy in a particular district, on that particular day. At La Rambla 87 there's a 24-hour pharmacy.

QUICK TIPS TO HELP YOU MANAGE YOUR MONEY

CREDIT CARDS Major cards like Visa, Mastercard or Maestro are widely accepted in restaurants, bars, hostels, train and bus stations and taxis. Always carry cash for minor transactions in small, traditional shops. American Express and Discover are not always accepted.

PAYING THE BILL
With a few exceptions (some takeaway cafes and local eateries), always expect to receive and pay the bill on the table.

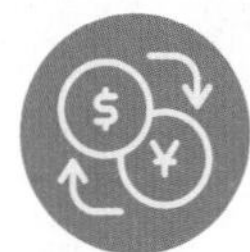

MONEY CHANGERS
Exchanging currency in banks is your best bet. Banks are open from 8am to 2pm.

CURRENCY

Euro

HOW MUCH FOR A...

Café con leche
€1.50

Caña
€2.50

Tapas lunch for two
€40

DISCOUNTS & SAVINGS

Most tourist attractions offer discounts to kids under 12 years, seniors and holders of ISIC cards. Discounts range from 30% to 50%.

Barcelona Card (barcelonacard.org) holders have unlimited metro and bus rides and get free entrance to museums and discounts at most tourist sites. Three-, four- and five-day passes cost €45, €56 and €61 respectively. Other bundle packs apply.

BARGAINING

Prices are always set, even in local markets, so bargaining is unheard of.

ATMS
All neighbourhoods and districts of Barcelona are heavily packed with banks and ATMs, and foreign credit cards are normally accepted. Caixabank is the most readily available.

TAXES & REFUNDS
VAT is 21% on most goods and services and 10% in hospitality; it is always included in the price. Foreigners are entitled to a 21% refund for purchases if they are taken out of the EU.

TIPPING

Restaurants Tipping is not mandatory, but locals tip as a reward for good service and food, typically leaving up to 5%. More than 5% is rare. Locals will tip by credit card, instead leaving spare change.

Bars For drinks, tips are not necessary, except for rounding off the final bill.

Taxis Taxi drivers don't expect tips from locals but, again, you can tip if you'd like to.

RESPONSIBLE TRAVEL

Positive, sustainable and feel-good experiences around the city

CHOOSE SUSTAINABLE VENUES

Visit an urban garden The city council has developed a set of urban vegetable gardens in almost every district. Some of them can be visited for free.

Relax at the garden of Olokuti One of the city's largest sustainable shops, Olokuti's store in Gràcia features an oasis city garden.

Stay in a green hotel Hostal Grau, for example, is a family-owned hotel whose furniture and decorations are made of sustainable materials; it even has an Off Room with an internet disabler.

Eat Km 0 Thrill your taste buds with locally sourced ingredients at places likec(traditional Catalan) or El Filete Ruso (burgers).

SOPA IMAGES/GETTY IMAGES ©

GIVE BACK

Collaborate on local social projects At miaportacion.org you can collaborate, donate and volunteer in countless local social projects, usually helping immigrants, people with disabilities or the elderly.

Donate your clothes Go light before leaving for home by donating your clothes in shops like the local NGO Humana, which recycles and gives a significant part of the donations to African countries. The rest is sold at their shops in Barcelona at very low prices. There are Humana shops in almost every neighbourhood.

Give jobs to the homeless Hidden City Tours (hiddencity-tours.com) employs homeless people as tour guides.

Above Volunteers distribute food with Barcelona City Council
Right Barceloneta beach
Far right Sant Andreu neighbourhood

LEARN MORE

Explore lesser-known neighbourhoods Sants, El Clot, Nou Barris, Sant Andreu and Horta Guinardó are local nueighbourhoods with almost no foreign visitors. They're packed with local eateries and a welcoming social life.

Attend festes del barri Each neighborhood has its annual cultural and folklore celebrations organised by residents; you can contribute to the local economy by attending.

LEAVE A SMALL FOOTPRINT

Sightsee by bicycle Barcelona is bike-friendly, and riding along Barceloneta promenade or the alleys of Barri Gòtic is a sustainable way to explore the city.

Hire a green taxi Taxi Ecològic is a local taxi app that only works with electric and hybrid taxis. By using this app, you also support local entrepreneurs.

PIOLA666/GETTY IMAGES ©

XAVI LAPUENTE/SHUTTERSTOCK ©

SUPPORT LOCAL

Eat local Each neighbourhood has its own local market where you can buy ingredients or dine at eateries cooking delicious food made with ingredients sold at the market.

Stay in registered accommodation Due to the increase in mass tourism and booking sites like Airbnb, many locals have been slowly pushed out from the old city. If you want to help fight this issue, stay in registered properties. The city council has launched a verifying tool, meet. barcelona.cat/habitatgesturistics/en, to help you find accommodation.

Buy local-made souvenirs Buy original souvenirs and gifts in shops like B de Barcelona or OMG BCN, which exclusively sell items made by artisans in Barcelona.

RESOURCES

barcelonasecreta.com
timeout.com/barcelona
turismesostenible.barcelona/en
nutricionsinfronteras.org

ESSENTIAL NUTS & BOLTS

GREETINGS

Spaniards are touchy-feely. Hugs and giving two kisses on the cheek when being introduced to someone or just to say hello is the norm.

SIESTA TIME

In local areas, shops close from approximately 2pm to 4.30pm for the most important meal of the day and its subsequent siesta.

BULLFIGHTING

There's no bullfighting in Catalonia; the regional parliament banned it in 2010.

FAST FACTS

GOOD TO KNOW

Drinking age The legal drinking age is 18.

Office hours
Spaniards finish work around 7pm or 8pm, the time when bars and shops get packed.

Visa information
Citizens of the EU and Iceland, Switzerland, Norway, the UK and Liechtenstein are just required to show their national ID to enter Spain. Nationals of countries like the USA, Australia, Canada, Japan, New Zealand or South Korea can get a 90-day free visa on arrival.

ACCESSIBLE TRAVEL

Generally speaking, Barcelona takes accessibility very seriously.

Tourist attractions and museums
All major sights are accessible, with ramps, elevators and adapted toilets. Audio guides and relief maps are mostly available as well.

Public transportation Except for 14 metro stations, all have elevators; all city buses have an access ramp and reserved spaces. The metro is accessible for the vision-impaired as well, with route indicators and guides in Braille available at information points. For further info, go to tmb.cat/en/barcelona/accessibility-mobility-reduced.

Taxi Taxi Amic (taxiamic.cat/en) is the local service for fully adapted taxis.

Hotels Larger hotels are mostly accessible, but not all. Double-check and book well in advance.

Wheelchair accessibility All street crossings have ramps and the medieval quarter is cobblestone free.

Beach access La Barceloneta beach has accessible paths.

SMOKING
Smoking is only prohibited in indoor public areas, like bars, restaurants and public institutions.

NOISINESS
Spaniards are extremely loud when talking, and love to interrupt each other. Get used to it.

PUNCTUALITY
Spaniards are not known for punctuality; be patient when waiting for a shop or bar to open.

FAMILY TRAVEL

Food *Tortilla de patatas, croquetas* and *calamares* are tapas local kids eat; some restaurants offer chicken nuggets or pasta with tomato sauce.

Bars It's common to see kids in bars, especially in terraces, around which occasional playgrounds have been built, like in Plaça del Sol (Gràcia) or Jardins del Dr Fleming (El Raval).

Prams A lack of cobblestones makes streets easy to navigate.

Activities Try Museu de la Ciència, Tibidabo Amusement Park, the Aquarium, the beach, Barcelona Zoo or Parc del Laberint d'Horta.

CATALAN & SPANISH

Both Catalan and Spanish have the same official status. Catalan is the language used by public institutions, but all Catalans are bilingual. In Barcelona, both cultures coexist and overlap, but learning some Catalan will prove that you care about the regional culture.

HAVE COFFEE LIKE A LOCAL

For breakfast, most locals order a *café con leche*, which is a big cup of coffee with milk. After meals (lunch and dinner), they normally order a *café*, which is essentially an espresso, or a *cortado*, an espresso with milk.

LGBTIQ+ TRAVELLERS

Spain was the fourth country to legalise same-sex marriage (in 2005).

Barcelona is super gay friendly Shows of affection in public are common and widely accepted.

'Gayxample' This area of l'Eixample is where many gay bars, clubs, restaurants, hotels and shops exist. Head to the area around carrer Consell de Cent 276, between Balmes and Compte d'Urgell.

Pride Barcelona Internationally acclaimed, this one-week festival hosts LGBTIQ+ events, such as concerts and parties.

LANGUAGE

Catalan and Spanish both have official-language status in Catalonia. In Barcelona you'll hear as much Spanish as Catalan, so we've provided some Spanish to get you started. Spanish pronunciation is not difficult for English-speakers, as most of its sounds are also found in English. You can read our pronunciation guides below as if they were English and you'll be understood just fine. And if you pronounce 'th' in our guides with a lisp and 'kh' as a throaty sound, you'll sound even more like a real Spanish person. To enhance your trip with a phrasebook, visit shop.lonelyplanet.com.

BASICS

Hello.	*Hola.*	o·la
Goodbye.	*Adiós.*	a·*dyos*
Yes./No.	*Sí./No.*	see/no
Please.	*Por favor.*	por fa·*vor*
Thank you.	*Gracias.*	*gra*·thyas
You're welcome.	*De nada.*	de *na*·da
Excuse me. (to get attention)	*Disculpe (pol)*	dees·*kool*·pe

What's your name?
Come si chiama? (pol) — ko·me see *kya*·ma
Come ti chiami? (inf) — ko·me tee *kya*·mee

My name is ...
Mi nombre es ... — mee *nom*·bre es ...

Do you speak English?
¿Habla inglés? — *a*·bla een·*gles*

I don't understand.
No entiendo. — no en·*tyen*·do

TIME & NUMBERS

What time is it?	*¿Qué hora es?*	ke *o*·ra es
It's (10) o'clock.	*Son (las diez).*	son (las dyeth)

morning	*mañana*	ma·*nya*·na
afternoon	*tarde*	*tar*·de
evening	*noche*	*no*·che
yesterday	*ayer*	a·*yer*
today	*hoy*	oy
tomorrow	*mañana*	ma·*nya*·na

1	*uno*	*oo*·no	**6**	*seis*	seys
2	*dos*	*doo*·e	**7**	*siete*	*sye*·te
3	*tres*	tre	**8**	*ocho*	*o*·cho
4	*cuatro*	*kwa*·tro	**9**	*nueve*	*nwe*·ve
5	*cinco*	*theen*·ko	**10**	*diez*	dyeth

EMERGENCIES

Help!	*¡Socorro!*	so·*ko*·ro
I'm ill.	*Estoy enfermo/a. (m/f)*	es·*toy* en·*fer*·mo/a
Call the police!	*¡Llame a la policía!*	*lya*·me a la po·lee·*thee*·a
Call a doctor!	*¡Llame a un médico!*	*lya*·me a oon *me*·dee·ko

Index

000 Map pages

000 Map pages

N

O

P

000 Map pages